WOW IT'S ALL A LOT

Samuel Leighton-Dore

Harper *by* Design

Foreword from Chris Cheers

'Rest, you beautiful, busy weirdo.'

This was the message I presented to my partner on his birthday. With these few simple words, Samuel and his beautiful tile did what they often do: they made my partner laugh, validated his experience and invited him to put his needs first.

This is the magic of these wondrous little tiles. They invite us to see things from a different perspective; not with pressure to feel better, but an invitation to look at things as they are.

The *Live, Laugh, Love* platitudes that Samuel's tiles so deftly satirise leave little space for the normal, difficult emotions that come up in life, and ask us instead to deny our emotional reality. It's not helpful to hear 'You've got this' when every part of you is telling you that you don't.

Samuel's words do something far more important. They teach us to view difficult emotions and challenges in life with kind curiosity – as difficult but temporary; hard but not overwhelming. Not to deny our discomfort, but to make space for it.

CARY T IS T IS JE?

DON'T HUSTLE SO HARD YOU FORGET TO ENJOY THIS WEIRD FUN LITTLE LIFE YOU'VE BUILT

WOW IT'S ALL A LOT HEY AT LEAST WE HAVE EACH OTHER

TOUCH FOR PROOF YOU EXIST

OLD YOU WOULD BE STOKED WITH PRESENT YOU

A- RDO

WOW IT'S ALL A LOT HEY AT LEAST WE HAVE EACH OTHER

TELL SOMEONE YOU LOVE THAT THEY'RE HOT SEXY SOFT GENTLE GONNA BE OK

REST YOU BEAUTIFUL BUSY WEIRDO

OUR LIGHT WON'T HIT THE STARS FOR ANOTHER HUNDRED YEARS

G IS O H- NOT TEAD

WOW IT'S ALL A LOT HEY AT LEAST WE HAVE EACH OTHER

YOUR THOUGHTS YOU

WOW IT'S ALL A LOT HEY AT LEAST WE HAVE EACH OTHER

IT REALLY IS ALRIGHT NOT TO HAVE AN OPINION ON EVERYTHING

S ME G ED

CHANCES ARE SOMEONE IS THINKING SOMETHING NICE ABOUT YOU RIGHT NOW

YOU ARE THE YELLOW BIT NOT THE PETALS

SOMETIMES IT'S GOOD TO TYPE IT OUT AND LEAVE IT IN DRAFTS

BIG THINGS GROW FROM SMALL THINGS EVENTUALLY. IT DOES TAKE AGES THOUGH.

S ME G D

WHAT OTHER PEOPLE THINK OF YOU ISN'T ALWAYS YOUR BUSINESS

EVEN IF THIS TILE BROKE IT WOULD BE BEAUTIFUL AND SO WOULD YOU

IS THAT THING WORTH WORRYING ABOUT OR COULD IT BE ADDRESSED IN THIRTY MINUTES?

THINGS TO LOOK FORWARD TO:

- YUMMY FOOD
- PRETTY SUNSETS
- KISSING STRANGERS

WOW IT'S ALL A LOT HEY AT LEAST WE HAVE EACH OTHER
YOUR BODY LOOKS STRON-G AND CAPA-BLE TODAY
TOUCH FOR PROOF YOU EXIST
WOW IT'S ALL A LOT HEY AT LEAST WE HAVE EACH OTHER
THAT SCARY THOUGHT IS REAL BUT IS IT TRUE?

Presenting these wonderful words on ceramic also adds to their ability to support. We all have some understanding of the time and skill it takes to create these beautiful objects from clay. And that understanding, I think, inspires us to appreciate the words at a deeper level. We are inspired to take a moment, slow down and process.

So, whether viewing the photographs in this book or holding a tile in your hand, it is also clear that these objects, whilst hard, are fragile in a way that beautifully echoes the emotional vulnerability Samuel is inviting us to be open to. People cannot show true empathy and support unless they know your experience, and people cannot know your experience unless you are willing to accept things as they are. And, just like each new layer of glaze, fired through the kiln, this vulnerability creates strength.

Samuel not only invites this helpful vulnerability but models it himself. In the essays presented with each tile, he offers the kind of wisdom that only comes from living through challenges, and the kind of validation and support that only comes from someone who is willing to share their struggle, especially when it is like the struggle you are also facing. I am certain you will have moments, just like I did, of reading Samuel's words and feeling so validated, because he has been where you are, and has made it through. His wisdom comes from a place of vulnerability and honesty. And therapy. Lots of therapy.

Samuel is not afraid to say, 'I am a work in progress. And that's okay.' Because we are all works in progress. All we can ever do, especially in times of trouble, is take each day as it comes and turn toward our emotions – even the most difficult – with compassionate curiosity. I think each tile encourages us to do this: to take that moment of bittersweet solace that comes from acknowledging the hard stuff but knowing it will be okay.

So, Samuel, to use your advice, let me tell you why I love you, 'in an uncomfortably specific way'. You share yourself to make us feel less alone. In a world of uncertainty, it can often feel like there is no safe place to rest our eyes. Your tiles, and this book, offer us this space.

So, thank you. You beautiful, busy weirdo.

Love, Chris

Chris Cheers is a psychologist, educator and author.

Introduction

I first started rolling out clay tiles and engraving words into them a few years ago, after I had just been diagnosed with complex post-traumatic stress disorder. Receiving the diagnosis was a huge relief – like, after years of pushing ill-fitting puzzle pieces together, I could finally see part of the reference image.

But my newfound clarity didn't change the fact that I was stuck in fight-or-flight mode, swinging back and forth like a metronome between panic and depression. I was also spending an increasing amount of time sitting in therapy waiting rooms, searching for meaning, encouragement, or even just a sign that I was in the right place or moving in the right direction. On the walls of those waiting rooms were photos of sprawling countryside landscapes, wild horses frozen mid-gallop and the occasional piece of driftwood with *Live, Laugh, Love* painted unironically in cursive.

I've always looked to art for orientation and meaning. My work is anchored in a need to understand who I am, but also why I am.

It's challenging work, peeling back all the layers of social conditioning and self-preservation in the hope of reaching some tender gravitational centre. And whenever I get close, I like to find the joy and humour in it. This process isn't always easy but, if approached with the right sense of tragic optimism, it can be kind of fun.

Enter: my Smile Tiles.

Despite the name, these tiles weren't born from a place of happiness. Much like the clay I use to make them, they are the result of an active excavation … in this case of myself. And, like their final ceramic forms, they represent a fragile imperfection that, I believe, connects and heals.

I began rolling out these earthenware tiles alone in my kitchen, etching phrases into them that I needed to hear. I never planned the phrases in advance, paying little mind to punctuation or where the words broke on each line (apologies to my editor). The words are earnest and sad, funny and optimistic, cathartic and connected to my experiences with mental health.

The tiles by no means represent how I live my life, but rather how I'd like to live it one day. Which is to say: they're aspirational but ultimately, I hope, relatable.

When I began sharing my tiles online, the response from friends and strangers alike was overwhelming, like I was being crushed by one of those hugs that just keeps going. Now, years later, over a thousand Smile Tiles hang on walls around the world – in homes, offices, recording studios, childcare centres, public bathroom walls ... and yes, even therapy waiting rooms, alongside those driftwood carvings and galloping horses.

It's the biggest honour to have a little piece of me in the lives of others, and I hope that this book can serve as a natural extension of an ongoing project that means so much to me. When you look through these pages, I hope you feel the sense of relief that comes from realising you're not alone in experiencing certain difficult thoughts and emotions. I hope you feel seen, and I hope it helps.

Because wow, life can be a lot sometimes ... but, hey, at least we have each other.

LOOK WHO'S:
-UP AND ABOUT
-GIVING IT A CRACK
-BEING CUTE

I reckon it's high time we started celebrating our bare minimum as the gold standard; holding 'life participation' certificates aloft with the same pride we might afford a first-place trophy. Because, with the world the way it is, it's pretty damn impressive to lug ourselves out of bed and give things a crack.

Culturally we tend to reward ourselves for achievements, recognising any effort only as it relates to a particular positive outcome. But, as I write this, sitting in a crowded bookshop café, I'm struck by how many people are up and about, showered [at least seemingly] and fully dressed, despite all the reasons not to be: burnout, fraught relationships, unfulfilling jobs, fragile mental health and financial stress. Yet here they are, walking around and engaging with the world. Some are even *smiling*.

Of course, all of this is relative; we face so many different kinds of suffering and personal setbacks, some objectively more challenging

We should all feel proud for putting one foot in front of the other, especially when the ground beneath us feels uneven and shaky.

than others. But we should all feel proud for putting one foot in front of the other, especially when the ground beneath us feels uneven and shaky.

So, please take this as the recognition you deserve. A new kind of affirmation, without the pressure of accomplishment. Because if you're reading this, you're up and about (or you have been recently). You're giving it a crack and I'm willing to bet that, even if you don't feel it, you're looking a little bit cute.

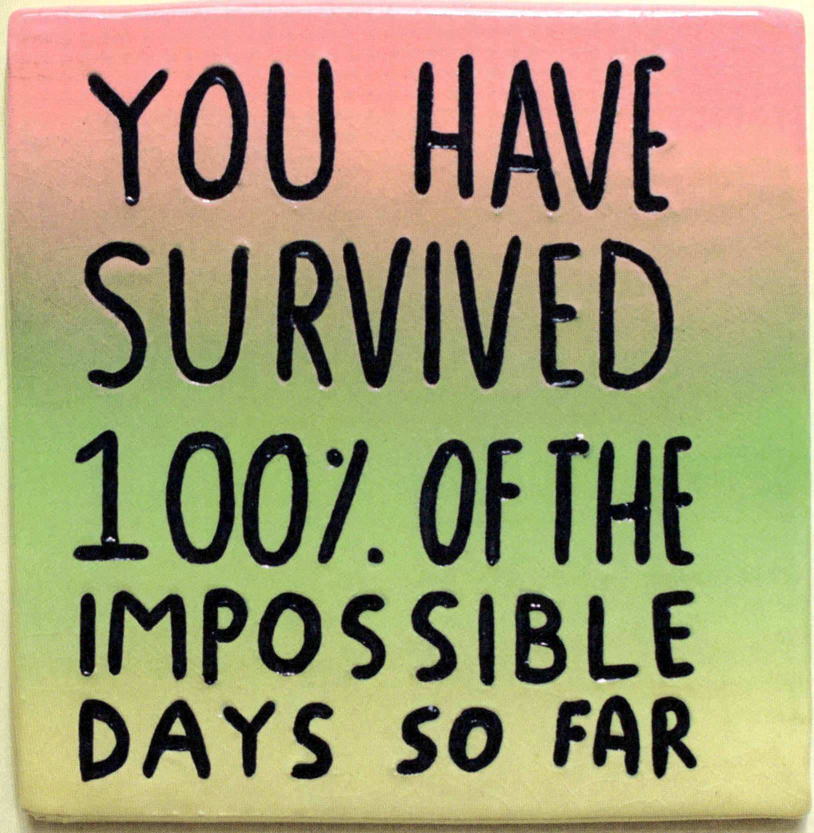

YOU HAVE
SURVIVED
100% OF THE
IMPOSSIBLE
DAYS SO FAR

Every time I'm having the kind of day that feels downright offensive, I like to take comfort in all the truly terrible days I've already made it through. Like the time I filmed a big Greek wedding and lost the memory card on the way home. Or the time I thought I'd found a bargain flight, but ended up boarding a plane to Santiago de los Caballeros, Dominican Republic, rather than Santiago del Estero, Argentina ... where my friends were waiting for me.

The good thing about having a shitty day is that every shitty day you make it through becomes evidence that you can survive future shitty days. As of now, you've persevered (in one way or another) through 100% of the seemingly impossible days since you involuntarily entered this world. So, when I say that you can get through this day, it's not me blowing smoke. It's a conclusion based on all the available information. It's not just that you can get through this – you almost certainly *will*.

We've all had terrible days, and we can look back on them to help give context to what we're experiencing in the present moment. Then, when it *feels* like they're going to break us, we can be unqualified statisticians about it and examine all the evidence to the contrary.

It's not just that you can get through this – you almost certainly *will*.

YOUR BODY
LOOKS STRON-
G AND CAPA-
BLE TODAY

My struggles with body image began, unoriginally, at my first school swimming carnival. I remember ogling the flat, muscled tummies of other boys my age as they lined up at the starting blocks, then looking down at the pretty little folds of my belly and willing them to disappear. The constant comparing of my body to others only accelerated from there. These ideas around how a body should look are fed to us early, often by media and advertising, and can be tricky to unlearn. As someone now in my thirties who definitely knows better, it's still a work in progress – but shifting my priorities and examining the language I use around my body has been a good start.

Concepts of strength and capability are entirely subjective, even in reference to the body. For someone living with chronic pain or illness, being able to comfortably walk around the block takes strength. For someone who requires support in day-to-day living, being able to sit up in bed and reply to a few work emails

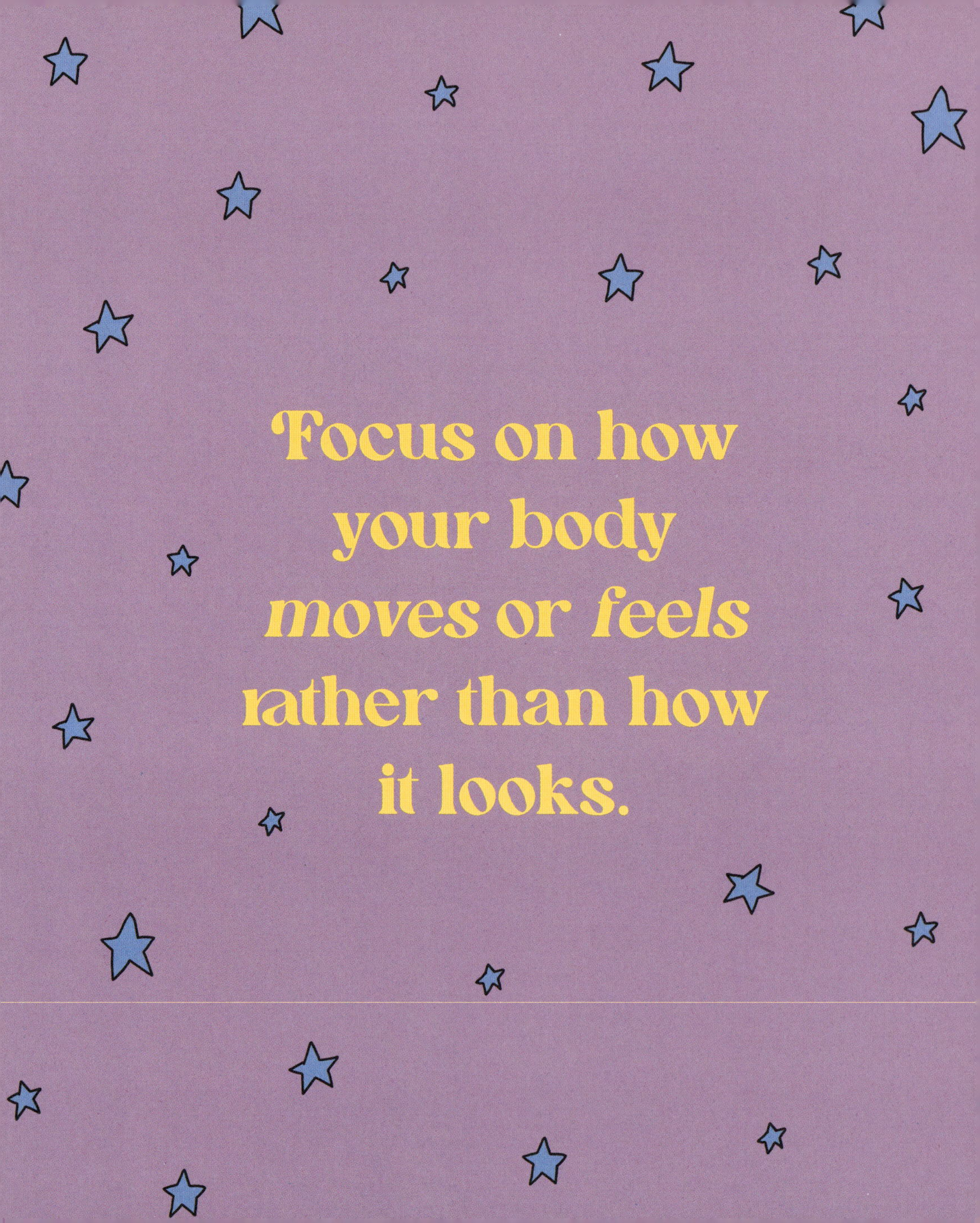
Focus on how your body *moves* or *feels* rather than how it looks.

demonstrates real-life capability. As a person who would rather jump out of a plane than engage in any form of interpersonal conflict, I can demonstrate resilience and strength by carrying myself through a difficult conversation without having a panic attack. I guess it always comes back to this: each and every body is beautiful, capable and strong in its own unique way, and there's no single metric for measuring these things. We get to make the metric.

In recent years, I've made a point of reconsidering my idea of 'strength' altogether, focussing on how my body *moves* and *feels* rather than how it *looks*. Again, everyone's different, but nurturing a new relationship with your body might involve tracking how much weight you can lift, rather than how much you weigh, or it might be even gentler than that. I think the goal should be to develop a mental flexibility, creating a healthier lens through which you perceive yourself and others.

DON'T HUSTL-
E SO HARD YO-
U FORGET TO E-
NJOY THIS WEI-
RD FUN LITTLE
LIFE YOU'VE BUILT

It's easy to subscribe to hustle culture. The very idea of it feels sleek, shiny and aspirational, as if the ability to burn the candle at both ends without scalding our fingers somehow elevates our status as a person. But isn't the word *hustle* just an exercise in sexy rebranding for 'allowing work to overtake our lives'?

My guess is that we are drawn to it because we're either chasing an elusive dream or achievement that we're convinced will make us happy, or running away from something (consciously or not) that we don't want to slow down long enough to examine. The problem I find with hustling is that it lends itself to more hustling. The more emails you send, the more emails you will get back, and the more you will have to reply to. ☹ Opportunities often lead to more opportunities. The very nature of hustle culture is cyclical and addictive and, before long, the risk of total mental and physical burnout becomes real.

One decidedly less-dramatic symptom of hustle culture is simply forgetting to enjoy our day-to-day lives. When we focus too much on our goals, we succumb to a kind of tunnel vision that blocks out all the little things in our periphery that make life special. We might forget to appreciate how lucky we are to have jobs, even if we're not passionate about them, or start to see social commitments as an inconvenience rather than a chance to connect and unwind. I'm pretty sure it's impossible to hustle and be present at the same time. And when we're not present, we forget to see our lives for what they are: weird and fun and, more often than not, the result of our own hard work.

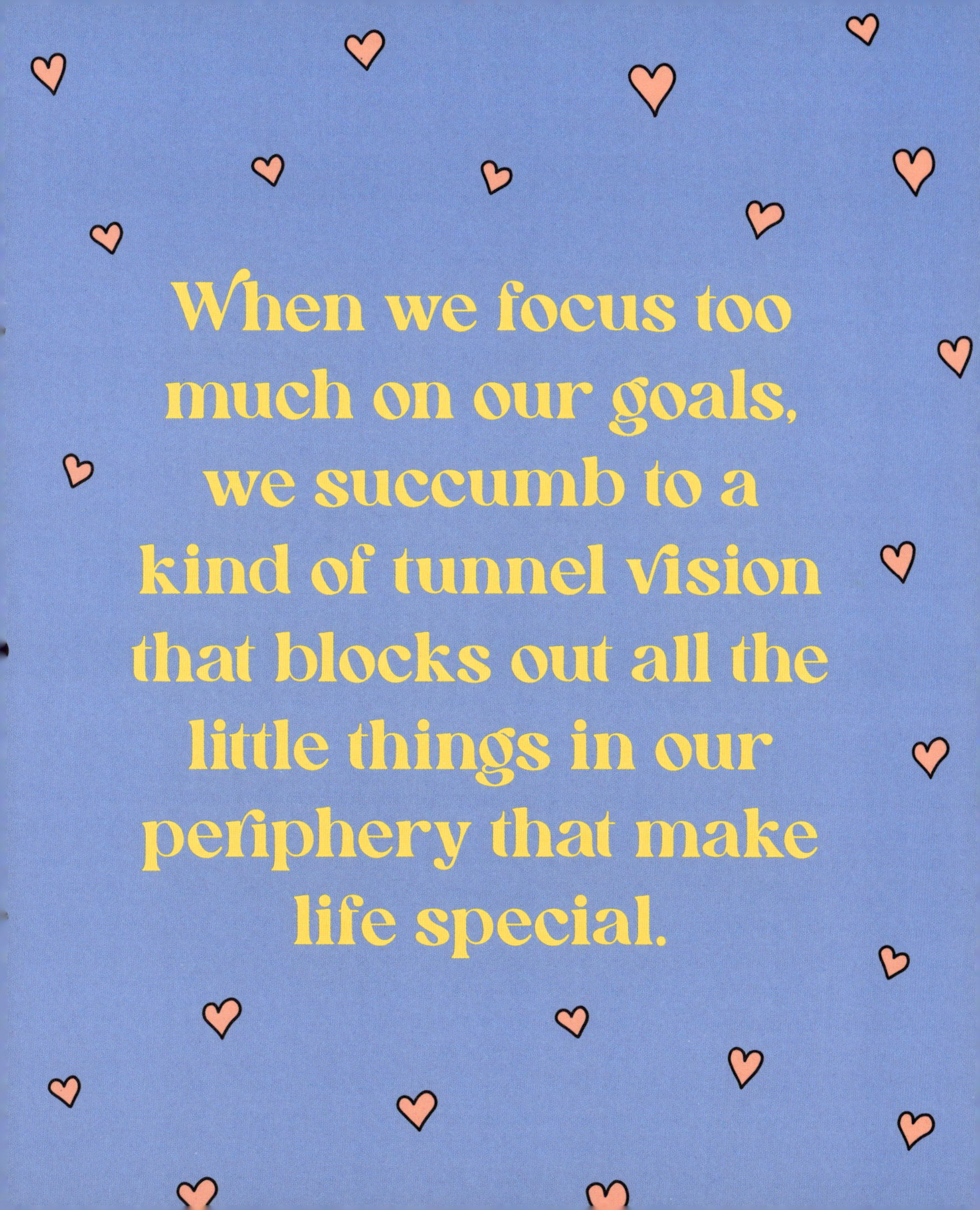

When we focus too
much on our goals,
we succumb to a
kind of tunnel vision
that blocks out all the
little things in our
periphery that make
life special.

EVERYTHING IS
ALREADY SO H-
ARD WHY NOT
BE SOFT INSTEAD

When I was fifteen, I emerged from a particularly challenging eight-year period in which I was repeatedly bullied. I felt heavy, like I was lumbering around in an ill-fitting suit of armour. I was clinking here, clanking there, knocking things over and leaving a trail of destruction everywhere I went. I knew that tears are to bullies what drops of blood are to sharks, so I did what I had been told to do for years: I toughened up and shielded myself with a mean sense of humour and an uncaring façade.

It's incredibly tempting to let the difficulties of life harden us, whether they be financial, emotional, psychological, existential, social, systemic, relational or something else entirely. And what makes life feel *extra* hard is that its obstacles are usually different for everyone, with precious little overlap in our shared experience of overcoming them. For instance, I used to think having more money would make my life easier ... and I'm sure it would, to an extent.

It's incredibly tempting to let the difficulties of life harden us.

But I've now met enough unhappy rich people to know that life just becomes hard in other less relatable ways.

It wasn't until I started therapy that I began to let myself soften, slowly lowering my guard and allowing myself to be vulnerable with friends and strangers. The thing about deciding to embrace life as a 'softy' is that it tends to catch on. When people see you bobbing along, all delicate and cracked open, you become a safe space for them to do the same. Over time, the friends and strangers I was vulnerable with began opening up to me too, resulting in many treasured bleary-eyed chats about our respective struggles and worries.

Acting with vulnerability and honesty is a low-key radical, empowering way to approach the world. Next time you engage with life's hardness, try remaining soft, despite your pointy edges.

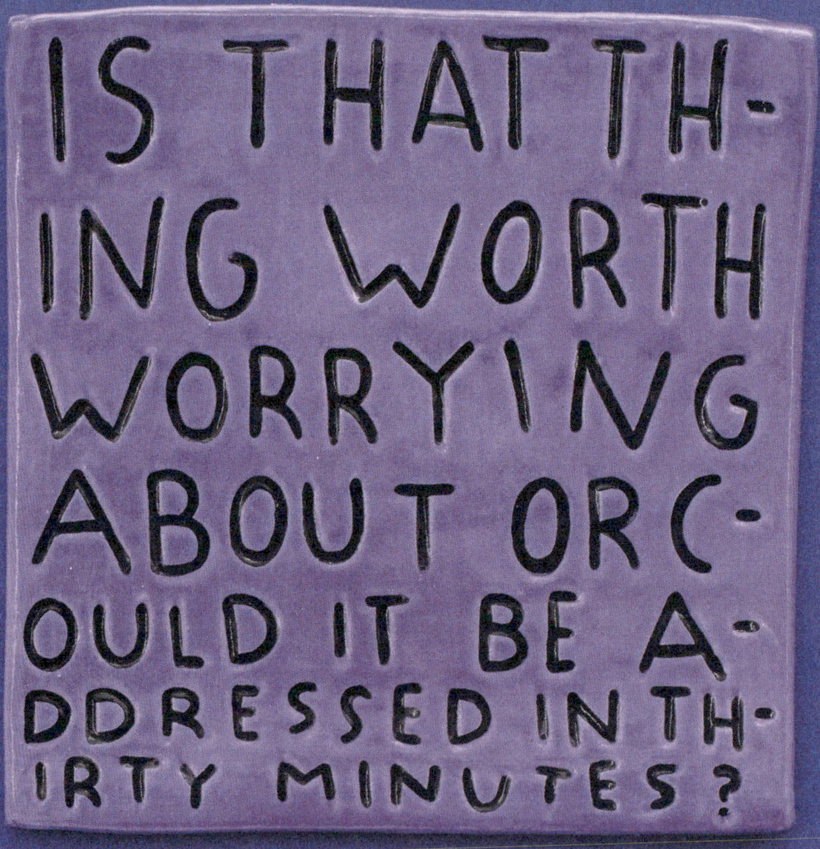

IS THAT TH-
ING WORTH
WORRYING
ABOUT OR C-
OULD IT BE A-
DDRESSED IN TH-
IRTY MINUTES?

Anyone living with ADHD will be intimately familiar with the dread of an unfinished task, but I'm sure it's something that everyone experiences on some level. For me, the idea of filling out any kind of official document makes me want to crawl under my bed, block my ears and wait patiently for rising water levels to reach my apartment. I'll ignore these tasks until they become a source of real anxiety, at which point they begin to feel much bigger than they actually are, and that only makes me avoid them more. If I had a dollar for every time I've left an important deadline to the very last minute because I felt so overwhelmed by a culmination of nonsense, I'd have ... a lot of money.

The irony is that many of the work/life things we worry about could probably be addressed within a reasonable timeframe of thirty minutes. Whether it's a form that needs filling out, an email that needs a response or a phone conversation that needs having, these are things that accumulate, overwhelm and keep us up at night. It's all so ... *unnecessary*.

Recently, when faced with one of these dreaded tasks, I tried to visualise myself thirty minutes into the future, with the task no longer hovering over me. It felt pretty good.

Taking a creative approach to the structure of a to-do list can help, too. Try one list for bigger, more time-consuming tasks, and one list for the nagging everyday stuff. I find that breaking them up into bite-sized pieces makes the list easier to digest, and setting clear priorities helps it all feel less like the final level in some tortured 'life admin' video game. The point is to get these tasks done, one baby step at a time.

Many of the work/life things we worry about could probably be addressed within a reasonable timeframe of thirty minutes.

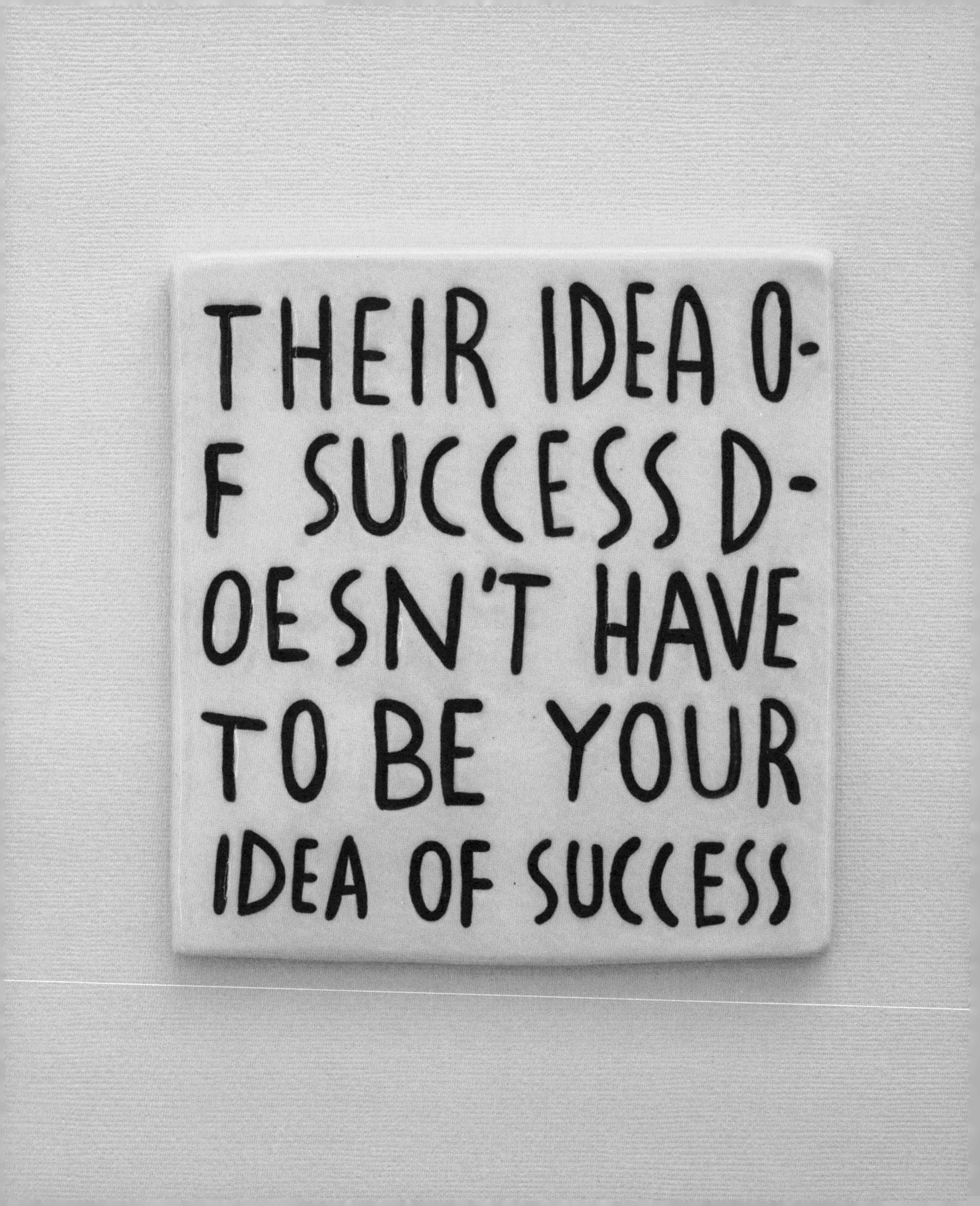

THEIR IDEA O-
F SUCCESS D-
OESN'T HAVE
TO BE YOUR
IDEA OF SUCCESS

I used to believe that I'd feel successful if I reached 10,000 followers on Instagram (cringe). Then I got there and I didn't feel … anything at all. Same with having a book published. Nada.

One pipe dream I hold, which I've recently discussed with my psychologist (Hi Susan, see you next Wednesday!) is to write an animated television series and win an Emmy. But I suspect that, in the unlikely event that both of these things happened, I'd walk off stage and feel an overwhelming sense of sadness, not success. In part this would be due to feelings of dread that I'd peaked, anxiety that I wasn't enjoying the moment as much as I should, and fear of what the audience was thinking of me. Hell, I'm already stressed about whether or not people will like this book, and I'm still writing it.

The way many of us think about success is insatiable. We're always moving the goalposts, robbing ourselves of any sense of achievement or celebration, while social media has us

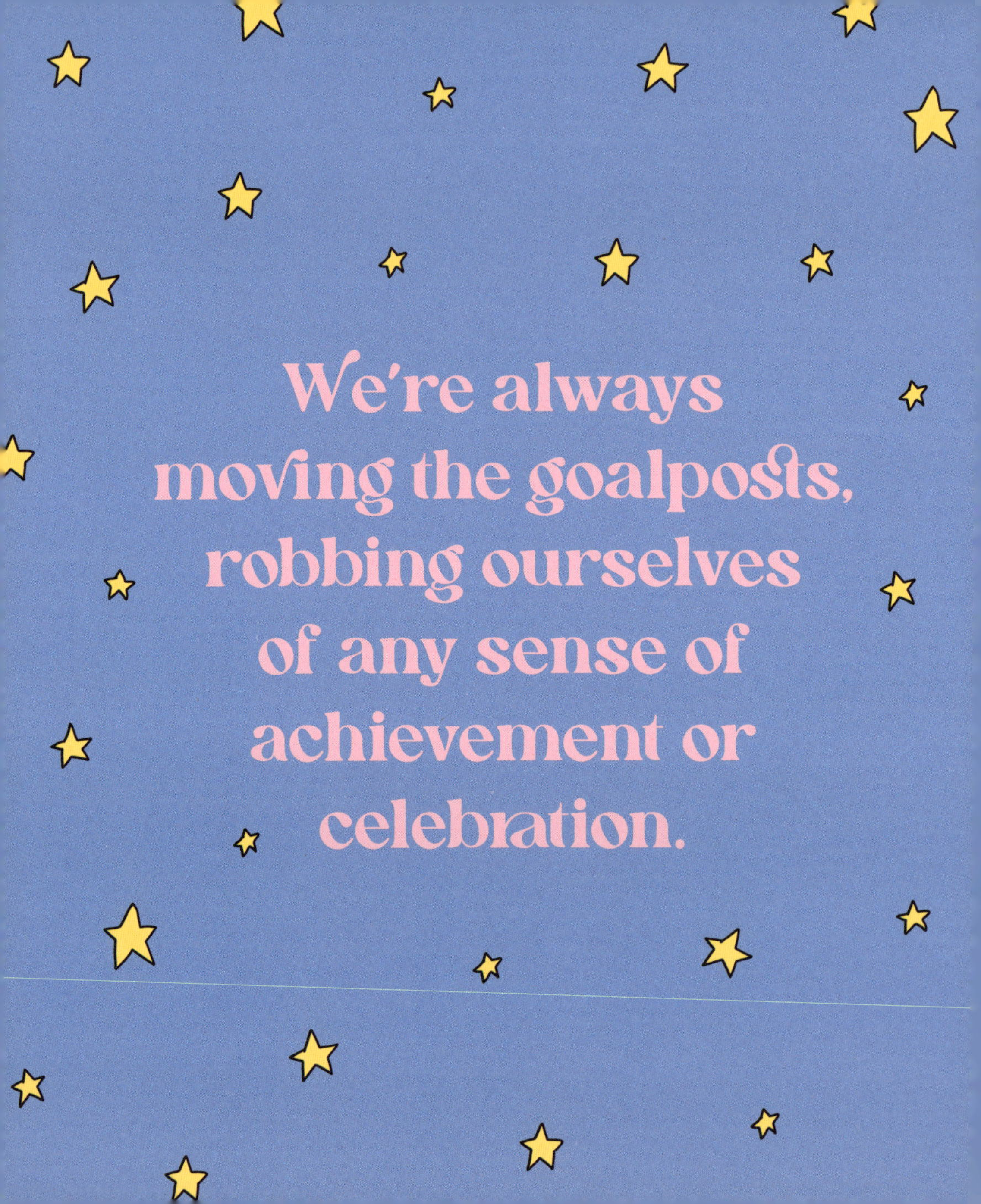
We're always moving the goalposts, robbing ourselves of any sense of achievement or celebration.

believing that likes + followers + the freedom to enjoy a casual European summer = success. It might just be me, but I can almost guarantee that if my biggest dream were to come true tomorrow, I'd still struggle to feel successful. Success isn't something to hang our happiness on, even if it is super shiny. Instead, remember why you placed those goalposts in the first place.

WHAT OTHER PEOPLE THINK OF YOU ISN'T ALWAYS YOUR BUSINESS

Caring about what other people think of me has always been my Achilles heel. I can trace it back to my struggle for acceptance throughout primary school, where five-year-old me had no point of reference for what made the 'cool kids' cool, and didn't understand why they wouldn't give me the time of day. The more they teased and isolated me, the more determined I became to seek their approval.

As I progressed into adulthood, the 'cool kids' took on different forms, but they still existed (in my mind, at least). I have been assured that it begins to bother you less as you age but, in the meantime, I'm trying to dig below that need for approval and examine what feeds it.

Trying to please everyone is a dead end, and trying to impress those who don't care for you only takes time away from connecting with those who do. You're better off staying in your own lane and focussing on the road ahead, rather than glancing sideways. Mind you, I use this metaphor as someone who still can't drive.

Trying to impress
those who don't care
for you only takes
time away from
connecting with
those who do.

WOW IT'S
ALL A LOT
HEY AT LEAST
WE HAVE
EACH OTHER

THAT SCARY THOUGHT IS REAL BUT IS IT TRUE?

It's quite common to have scary thoughts in daily life – I have had my fair share. I could be bushwalking and think, 'What if I jumped off this cliff, hitting every jagged rock on the way down?', or I'll be in the passenger seat of a car and think, 'What if I grabbed the steering wheel and turned us into oncoming traffic?' These thoughts are violent and scary and don't really deserve to be reasoned with, which is why I find comfort in the differentiation between what is 'real' and what is 'true'.

Consider the question, 'Am I a murderer?' Objectively speaking it is *real* because I just thought and wrote it down, but it's also *untrue* because I've never murdered anyone or genuinely considered it. Still, nobody has managed to invent a security system for the human brain yet, and anyone who's been stopped in their tracks by a scary 'What if?' thought knows how hard they can be to ignore and tune out.

I find comfort in
the differentiation
between what is
'real' and what
is 'true'.

Try to think about scary thoughts like thriller films. They're *real* in the sense that we experience them and can be genuinely affected by them, but they're *untrue* in the sense that they're just a story. In the same way a film crew huddles behind the camera to create an illusion for their audience, these shock-jock thoughts are just produced by our psyches to distract and, if we let them, entertain us.

TOUCH FOR
PROOF YOU
EXIST

Those who have pulled in at 'Dissociation Station' know how unsettling it can be to feel outside of your body and detached from reality. I imagine it's a little like coming out of a coma, except you're at a family dinner and it's your turn to talk.

Luckily our senses can help to ground us. Touch doesn't have to be your love language to be helpful. One thing my mum has suggested is to go outside, pick up a dry leaf and scrunch it up, feel it crackle, then watch it break apart and fall to the ground.

Another common way of approaching this sensory exercise is by quietly listing five things you can see (people eating breakfast, a barista taking someone's coffee order, a notification that my phone battery is running out of charge, a stranger's toddler plopping themself down on the floor in protest, an elderly woman scratching her Scratchie with a ten-cent coin);

four things you can feel (the cushioned seat I'm sitting on, the keys beneath my fingers as I type, my left leg crossed over my right knee, a little bit of anxiety churning away in my stomach); three things you can hear (a shop assistant laughing with a customer, a family chatting nearby, early 2000s pop music playing over a distant speaker); two things you can smell (I've got almost no sense of smell so I skip this one); and one thing you can taste (the long black coffee I've been slowly sipping for the past two hours, despite it having long gone cold).

Touch doesn't have to be your love language to be helpful.

IS IT ACTUA-
LLY URGENT
OR IS YOUR A-
NXIETY TR-
ICKING YOU?

My apartment smoke alarm goes off every time the temperature rises above 25°C, and I'm based in Queensland so that's almost every day. I live in constant anticipation of the shrill siren; it wakes me up in the middle of the night and makes me feel like I'm losing my mind.

In my experience, this is what living with chronic anxiety is like: everything feels higher stakes than it really is and everyday challenges are laced with a disproportionate sense of danger or doom. It becomes difficult to discern situations that are *actual* emergencies from those that are simply triggering your brain's faulty warning systems.

When it comes to work-related tasks or life admin, this can become particularly tricky. Emails feel urgent. To-do lists feel urgent. Social media inboxes feel urgent. And, when everything feels equally overwhelming, we end up ignoring the stuff that actually *is* urgent.

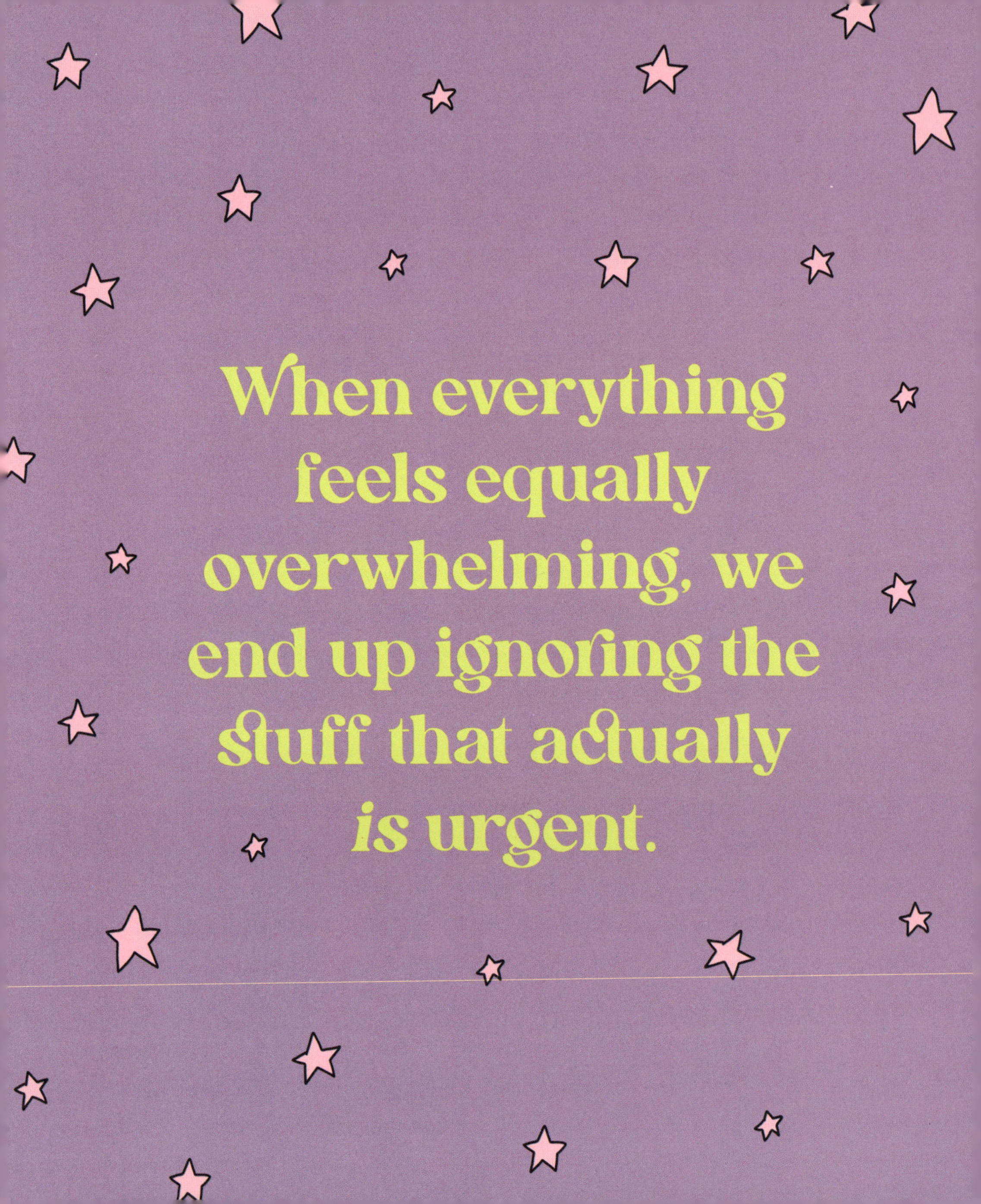
When everything feels equally overwhelming, we end up ignoring the stuff that actually is urgent.

Anxiety is very good at tricking us into thinking that we're supposed to be doing a million things all at once, rather than one or two key things at a time. Add to that how accessible we've all become with our devices and you can see how the problem becomes easily compounded.

However, the next time you feel overwhelmed, try pausing and asking yourself: 'Is there evidence to support my brain's sense of urgency?' Taking this moment to check in might help you focus on whatever it is you need (or want) to be doing instead.

SOMETIMES
IT'S GOOD T-
O TYPE IT OU-
T AND LEAVE
IT IN DRAFTS

I'm going to start with one of my trademark deep guttural sighs. *S-I-G-H.*

Learning to *respond* instead of *react* is something of an ongoing journey for me. An example I heard on a podcast recently is finding a dog alone in the forest and trying to pat it, only for it to bark at you aggressively. You might scream in fear and start to retreat, but then realise one of its paws is stuck in a trap and that the bark was due to pain, not aggression. (Thanks Tara Brach!)

I think we've all been that dog at one point or another. Whenever I receive an email that upsets me for some reason, my instinct is to bark back with a defensive or borderline passive-aggressive email, signed off with 'Best, Sam'. I've clicked 'send' on some doozies in my professional life and have never once gone to bed feeling good about it.

I've learned instead that this a pretty good time to step away from my keyboard and pause.

More often than not, the rejection or criticism is only upsetting me because it reinforces one of my self-beliefs (for example, that I'm the most embarrassing flop since that original member of The Beatles who was fired) or triggers a memory of some deeply buried childhood experience of rejection, criticism, abandonment or defectiveness.

You could try running your draft response past a non-judgemental friend or group chat to help edit it down to something more measured and less emotional. Sometimes you just need to type it out and have those raw, reactive feelings validated by people you trust, and sometimes you don't even need to send the response at all. That pause between *feeling* and *doing* is where we have some power to control the narrative and outcome, especially if we don't like the direction it's heading in. Put it down in drafts as 'Email (Taylor's Version)' and sleep on it. You'll thank yourself later.

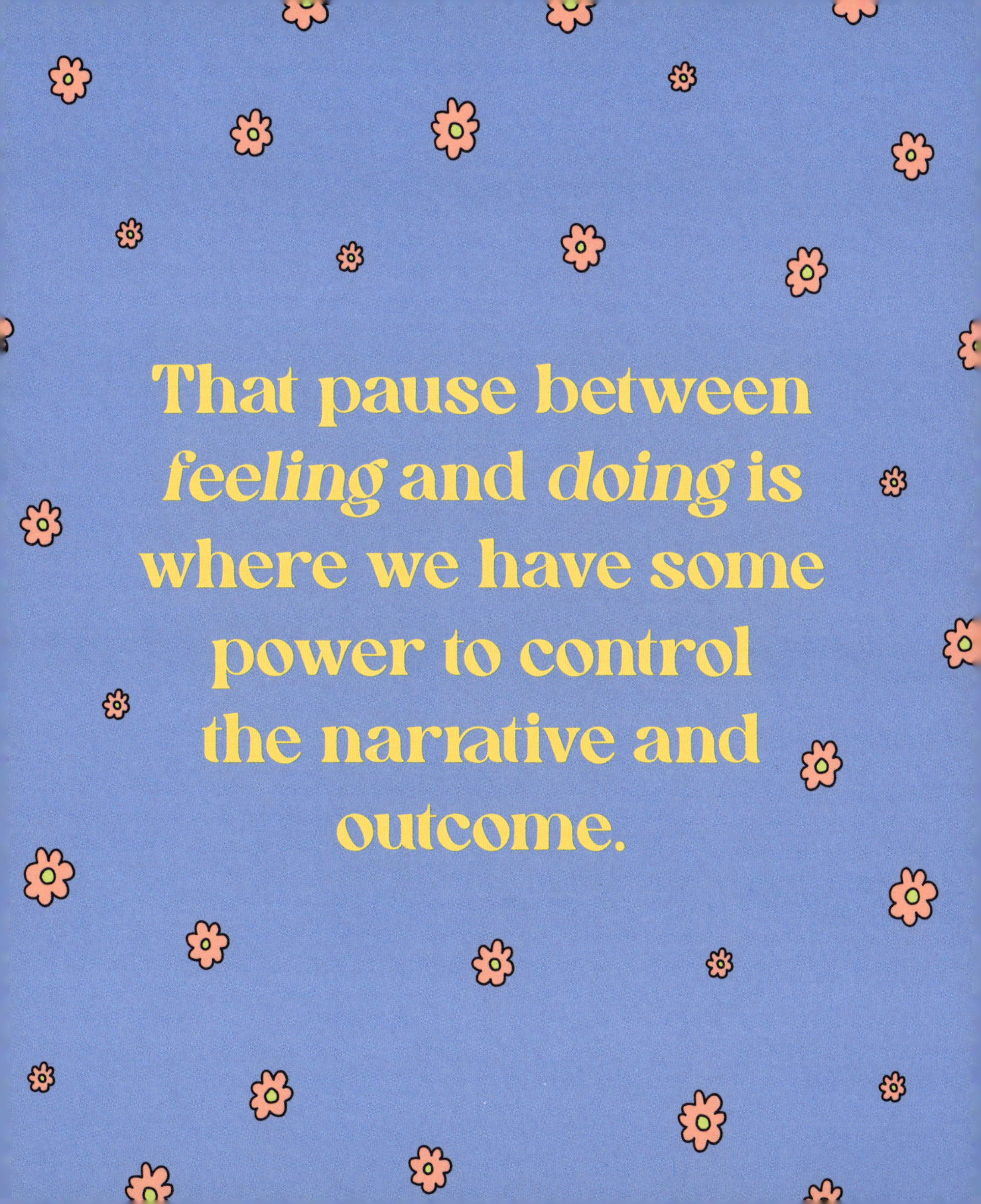
That pause between
feeling and *doing* is
where we have some
power to control
the narrative and
outcome.

YOU DON'T
HAVE TO
READ THE
NEWS TODAY

During the first year of the pandemic I found myself (along with most everyone else) hooked to the news like it was a daily oxygen tank. I followed every single tedious update until it became my main source of anxiety, distraction and (in a messed-up way) entertainment. At one stage, I could've easily ranked each state-based sign-language translator by how hot, funny, well-dressed or engaging they were.

There's just so much news these days and it breaks so often you'd be forgiven for thinking it's broken. There's war, poverty, politics, corporate fraud, corruption, the climate emergency and entertainment gossip. It's all a lot and, while it's obviously important to stay informed, we can't really be expected to keep up with it, especially when elements can be traumatic or triggering.

I had to start setting some boundaries (we love a boundary!), starting with dedicated 'no news'

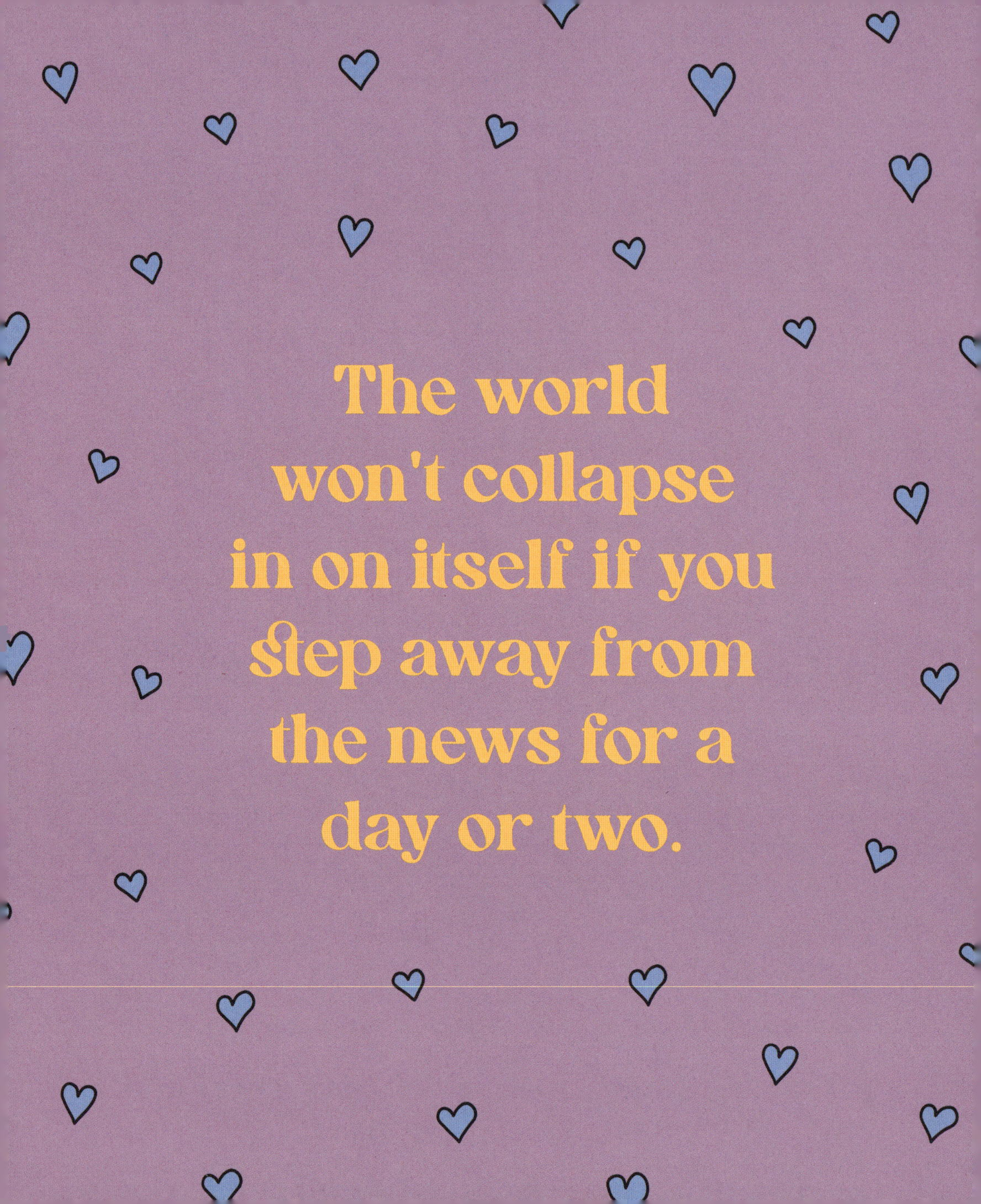
The world
won't collapse
in on itself if you
step away from
the news for a
day or two.

days. I also turned off my news-app notifications and restricted my consumption to one trusted source or publication. I don't think I'm any less informed now. If anything, my engagement with the news has become more intentional, which helps me form measured responses while looking after my wellbeing.

The world won't collapse in on itself if you step away from the news for a day or two. If something urgent *does* happen, someone is probably going to let you know anyhow, whether or not you're watching it happen live. Because, at the end of the day, the news is always moving and sometimes we just need to be still.

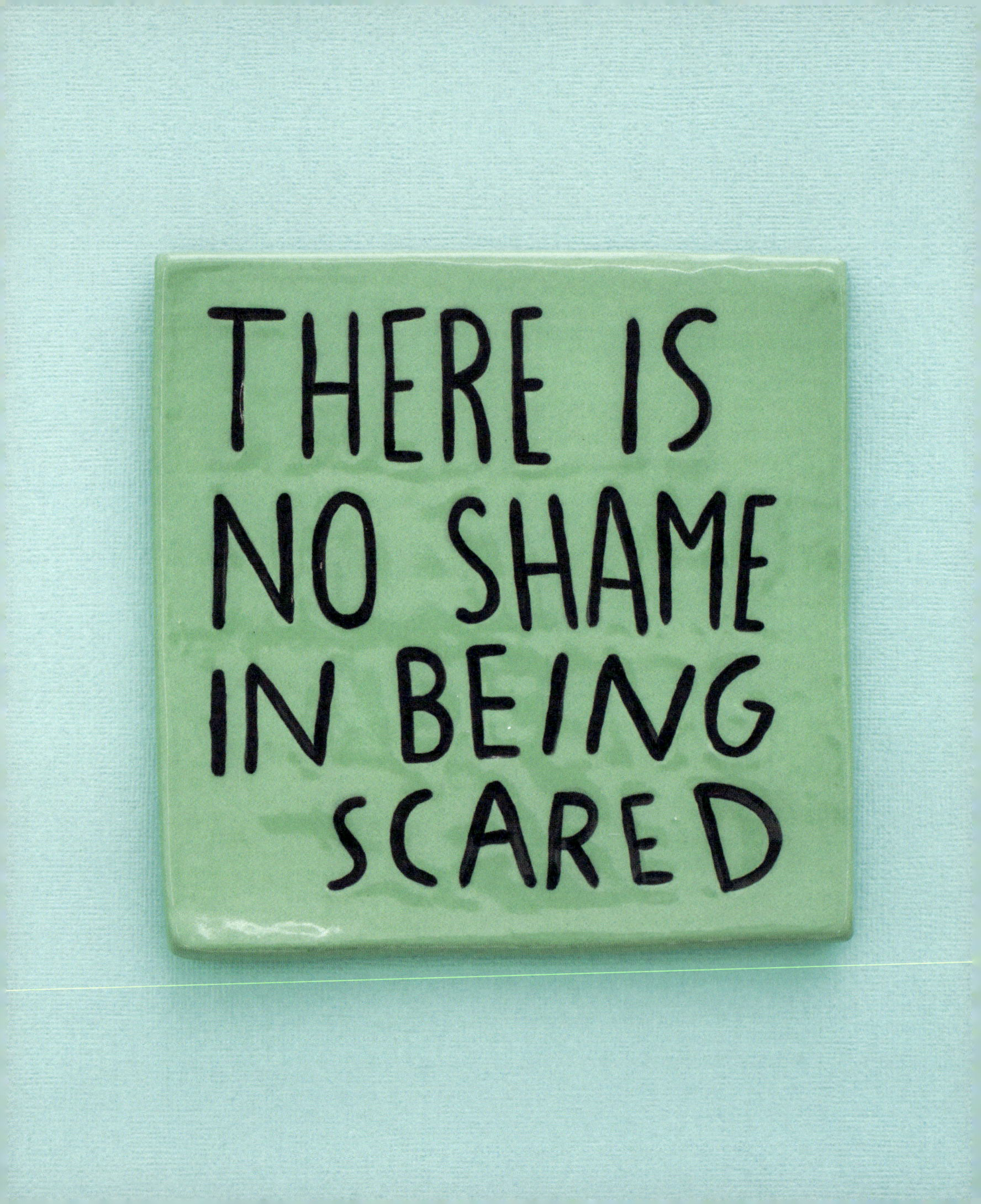

THERE IS NO SHAME IN BEING SCARED

I really wish humans could be more open about how damn scared we are all the time. Most of us are scared of ageing, scared of death, scared of not being good enough, scared of climate change … the list is endless.

So many of the emotions and behaviours we express on a daily basis are fear-based, yet we somehow continue to look at fear as a sign of weakness – particularly in the case of men (sorry men, I love you!). The thing about fear is that, when we're open about it with others, it has an ability to help form healthy connections. It's hard not to feel a little relieved every time another person admits they're scared of the same things you are – and this shared experience has huge potential to bring us together in a positive way.

Fear is only a problem when we push it down and let it bubble up as secondary emotions: shame, anger, defensiveness and irritation, to name a few.

Take, for example, bullying in the schoolyard or workplace. In one way or another, nearly all bullying boils down to an innate fear of not being loved or accepted. If unexpressed, this fear can manifest as deep insecurity, which might in turn compel us to assert our social standing by putting others down. It's not like Regina George was *born* a mean girl. Her emotional needs as a kid probably weren't met, so she adapted to fit her mum's shallow value system and became a screen on which to project her parent's unfulfilled needs and desires. In all likelihood, Regina and Cady were navigating the same fear of not belonging – they just processed it in different (and then ultimately similar) ways.

We often say that hurt people *hurt* people, but scared people scare people too. So, let's lean into the collective strength that can be found in gently sharing, not hiding, our fears and vulnerabilities.

It's hard not to feel a little relieved every time another person admits they're scared of the same things you are.

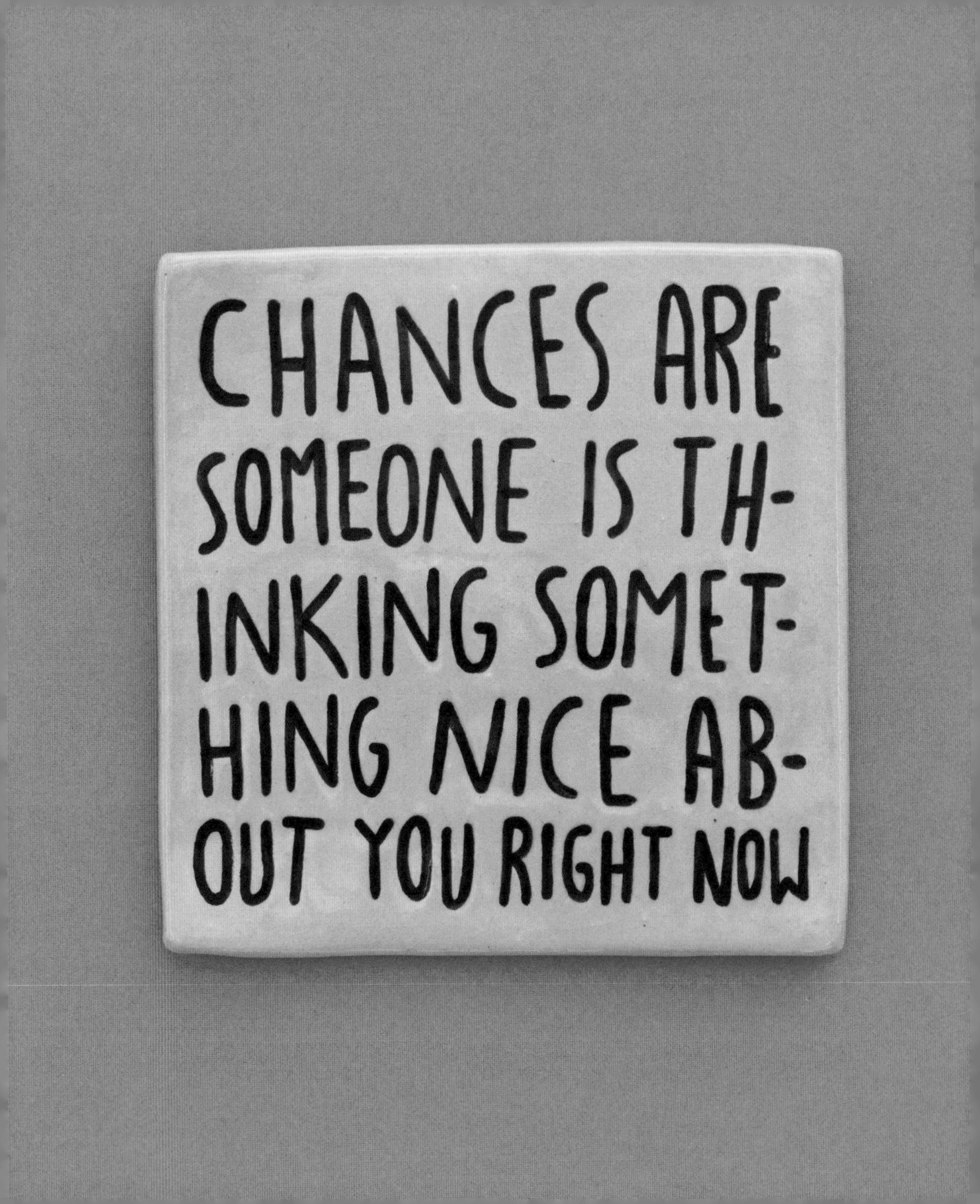

CHANCES ARE
SOMEONE IS TH-
INKING SOMET-
HING NICE AB-
OUT YOU RIGHT NOW

I often find myself convinced that people don't like me. I might imagine that, after every phone call or work Zoom, the person on the other end immediately says something negative about me to whomever they're with in real life. Or that whenever I leave a room there's a collective sigh of relief, like everyone has been quietly counting down the minutes until they could escape my presence.

This might all sound irrational, but I suspect variations of these thoughts are more common than we think. If we see ourselves as unworthy of love or belonging, then when those positive emotions are openly expressed to us, we feel suspicious. It's like we're on *Survivor* and expecting some humiliating post-merge blindside. This is why we place so much more meaning on overhearing something nice said about us, than when someone says it to our face. It gives us permission to believe that the words are truthful and not just a performance.

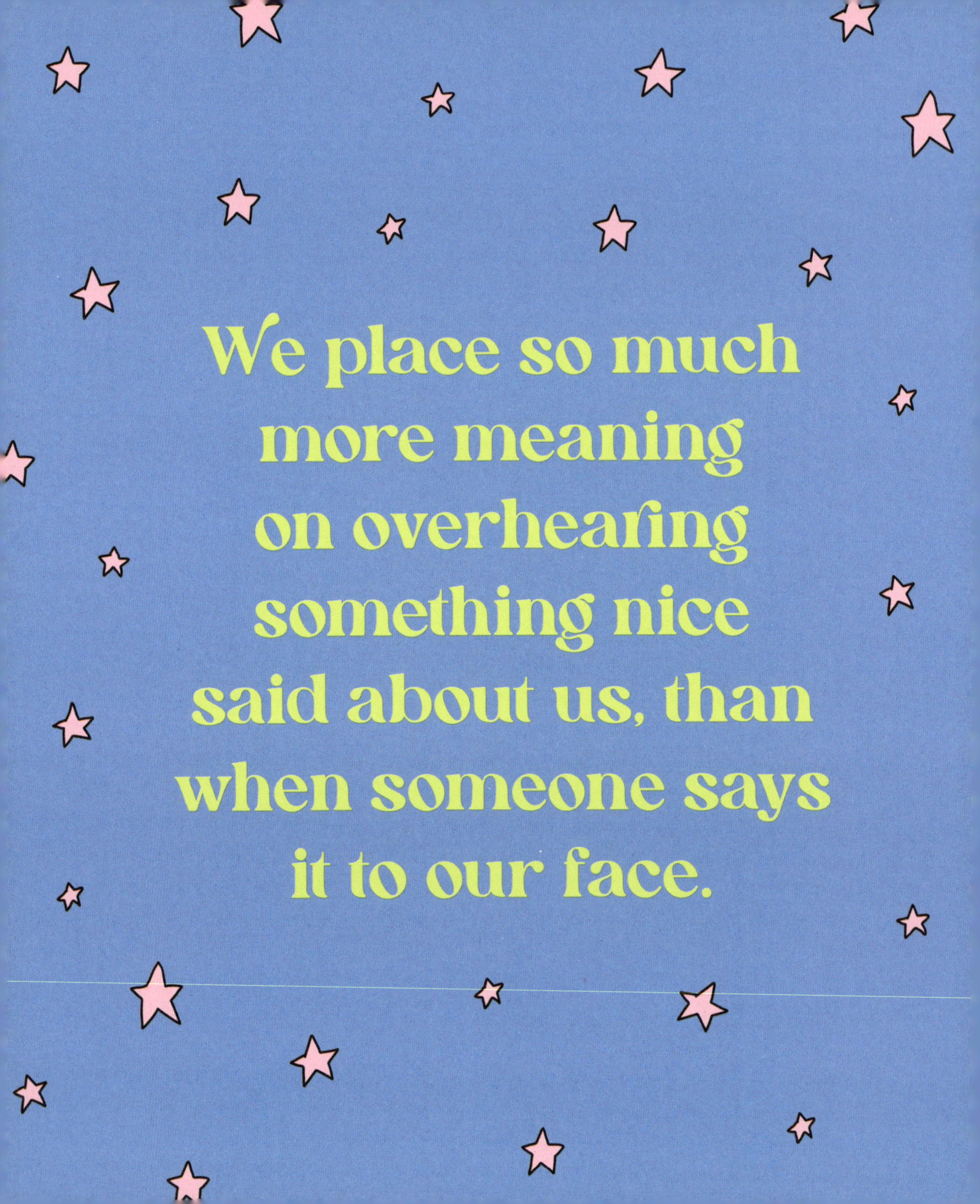
We place so much
more meaning
on overhearing
something nice
said about us, than
when someone says
it to our face.

It's much easier to imagine people thinking nasty thoughts about us than nice ones. Because so many of us are already caught up thinking nasty thoughts about ourselves. But the reality is that there are probably people thinking nice thoughts about you right now. Or there might've been yesterday. Or maybe there will be tomorrow. It does happen!

At one point or another you would've shared real belly laughs with someone, or supported them through a difficult time, or listened openly and without judgement as they filled you in on their favourite *Real Housewives* franchise. Nobody forgets that stuff. They store it up in a metaphorical 'when I need it' folder to revisit on tough days. And whether they tell you or not (they usually won't), they'll think how nice it was that you showed up for them.

TELL SOMEONE
YOU LOVE THAT
THEY'RE HOT S-
EXY SOFT GEN-
TLE GONNA BE OK

One hill I'll gladly die on is the notion that we don't spend enough time getting disgustingly earnest with our compliments. We might tell a friend they look good, send a fire reaction to their Instagram story or make nice, encouraging comments about whatever project they've been working on. But in an emoji-littered landscape it can become increasingly difficult for us to express in actual words what we love most about each other, because being earnest is seen as cringe-worthy, saccharine and, perhaps worst of all, uncool.

Instead, we delegate most of what we'd like to say to subtext, hoping others pick up on the I-love-you-so-much-I'd-honestly-die-for-you vibe without having to explicitly vocalise it. But when we tell someone what we love about them in an uncomfortably specific way, it makes them feel good. And when they feel good, we feel encouraged to do more of whatever it was that made that happen.

Perhaps embracing things that make us cringe is precisely what we're missing in our lives? How would our relationships change if we spent more time telling our friends that we needed them or that they're special to us? That we love how hot, sexy, soft and gentle they are, and that, despite the unending barrage of bad news we encounter every day, chances are they're going to be okay? I reckon we'd probably all feel a little more seen, a little more appreciated, a little more loved and a little less alone. And, if that's the case, being uncool is a small price to pay.

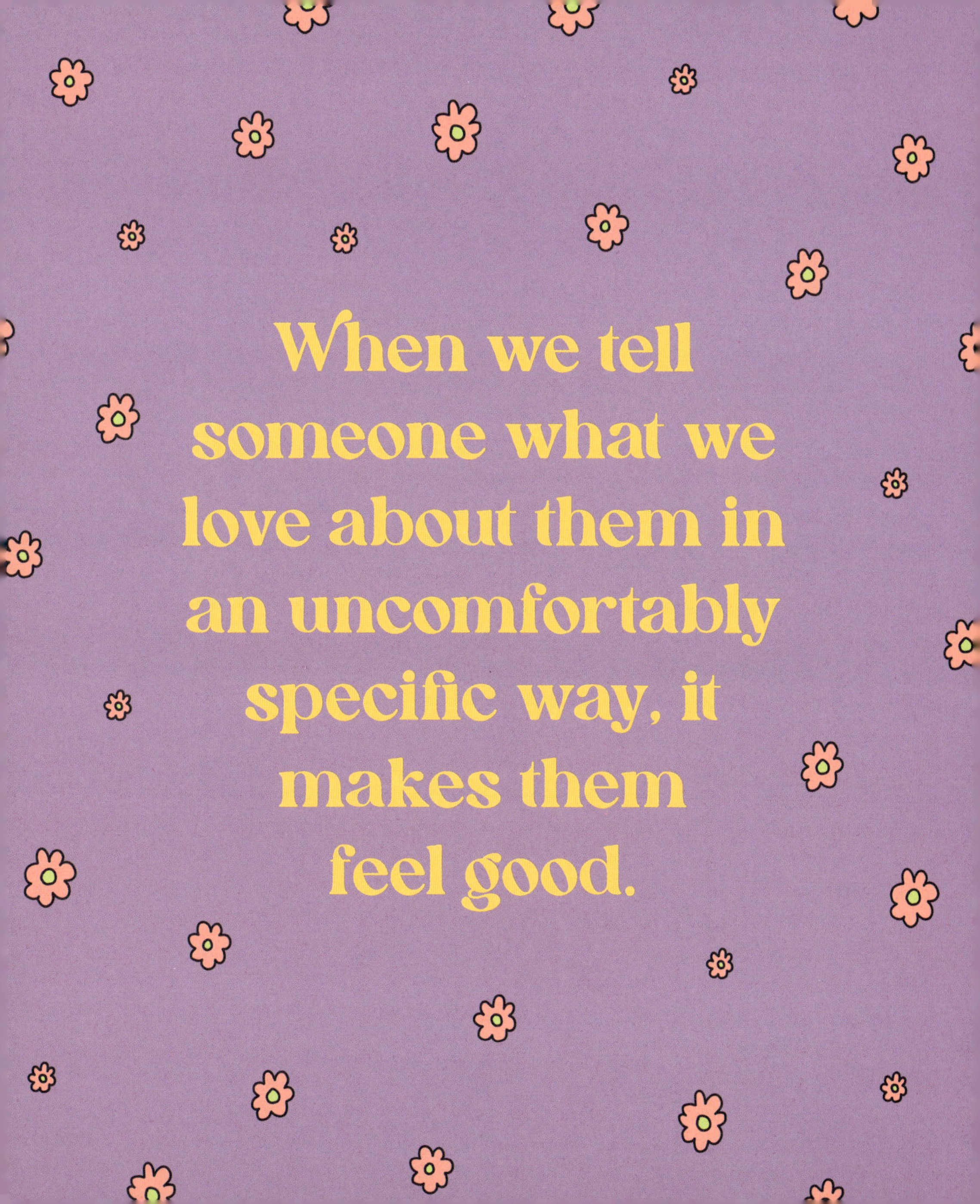
When we tell someone what we love about them in an uncomfortably specific way, it makes them feel good.

YOU EXIST BEYOND Y-OUR CIRCU-MSTANCES

YOU CAN DO IT* *GET THRO-UGH THIS DAY

YOUR BODY LOOKS STRON-G AND CAPA-BLE TODAY

LOOK WHO'S:
- UP AND ABOUT
- GIVING IT A CRACK
- BEING CUTE

THA THO REAL IT

YOUR THOUGHTS ≠ YOU

YOU DON'T HAVE TO READ THE NEWS TODAY

THAT SCARY THOUGHT IS REAL BUT IS IT TRUE?

NOT EVERY CLOUD HAS A SILVER LI-NING AND THAT IS OKAY

RE YOU UTI BUSY

YOU CAN DO IT* *GET THRO-UGH THIS DAY

WOW IT'S ALL A LOT HEY AT LEAST WE HAVE EACH OTHER

THEIR IDEA O-F SUCCESS D-OESN'T HAVE TO BE YOUR IDEA OF SUCCESS

HAHAHAHA HAHAHAHA HAHAHAHA HA OH DEAR

EVER ALRE ARD BE SO

OLD YOU WOULD BE STOKED WITH PRE-SENT YOU

LOOK AT YOU YOU WONKY BIG STAR

OUR LIGHT WON'T HIT THE STARS F-OR ANOTHER HUNDRED YEARS

CARE M-ORE MI-ND LESS

THE NO IN E

DON'T HUSTL-E SO HARD YO-U FORGET TO E-NJOY THIS WEI-RD FUN LITTLE LIFE YOU'VE BUILT

TELL SOMEONE YOU LOVE THAT THEY'RE HOT S-EXY SOFT GEN-TLE GONNA BE OK

IS IT ACTUA-LLY URGENT OR IS YOUR A-NXIETY TR-ICKING YOU?

IF YOU CAN RE-AD THIS YOU A-RE NO LONGER A BABY BUT Y-OU'RE STILL LOVED

THE NO IN B SC

DON'T HUSTLE SO HARD YOU FORGET TO ENJOY THIS WEIRD FUN LITTLE LIFE YOU'VE BUILT

WOW IT'S ALL A LOT HEY AT LEAST WE HAVE EACH OTHER

TOUCH FOR PROOF YOU EXIST

OLD YOU WOULD BE STOKED WITH PRESENT YOU

WOW IT'S ALL A LOT HEY AT LEAST WE HAVE EACH OTHER

TELL SOMEONE YOU LOVE THAT THEY'RE HOT SEXY SOFT GENTLE GONNA BE OK

REST YOU BEAUTIFUL BUSY WEIRDO

OUR LIGHT WON'T HIT THE STARS FOR ANOTHER HUNDRED YEARS

WOW IT'S ALL A LOT HEY AT LEAST WE HAVE EACH OTHER

YOUR THOUGHTS

YOU

WOW IT'S ALL A LOT HEY AT LEAST WE HAVE EACH OTHER

IT REALLY IS ALRIGHT NOT TO HAVE AN OPINION ON EVERYTHING

CHANCES ARE SOMEONE IS THINKING SOMETHING NICE ABOUT YOU RIGHT NOW

YOU ARE THE YELLOW BIT NOT THE PETALS

SOMETIMES IT'S GOOD TO TYPE IT OUT AND LEAVE IT IN DRAFTS

BIG THINGS GROW FROM SMALL THINGS EVENTUALLY IT DOES TAKE AGES THOUGH.

WHAT OTHER PEOPLE THINK OF YOU ISN'T ALWAYS YOUR BUSINESS

EVEN IF THIS TILE BROKE IT WOULD BE BEAUTIFUL AND SO WOULD YOU

IS THAT THING WORTH WORRYING ABOUT OR COULD IT BE ADDRESSED IN THIRTY MINUTES?

THINGS TO LOOK FORWARD TO:

- YUMMY FOOD
- PRETTY SUNSETS
- KISSING STRANGERS

WOW IT'S
ALL A LOT
HEY AT LEAST
WE HAVE
EACH OTHER

It's been a big few years for wildly gesturing at everything and swearing. Optimism is out and existential dread is in. We're stuck oscillating between bushfire and flood seasons, watching white men in suits continue to bend global politics towards violence and inequality, slowly letting go of our dreams of home ownership, and nervously navigating a global pandemic. It feels like there's no safe place to rest our eyes or ears.

Despite this, there is comfort to be found in linking arms with your fellow humans and looking deep into the abyss together. If misery loves company, then a justifiable fear about the future of humanity does too. Even if there were a deadly comet hurtling towards us, wouldn't the group chats be fun? Wouldn't the memes make us laugh through the fear? Wouldn't our shared experience ease the dread?

This might all sound very macabre, but I believe in acknowledging just how tough everything is

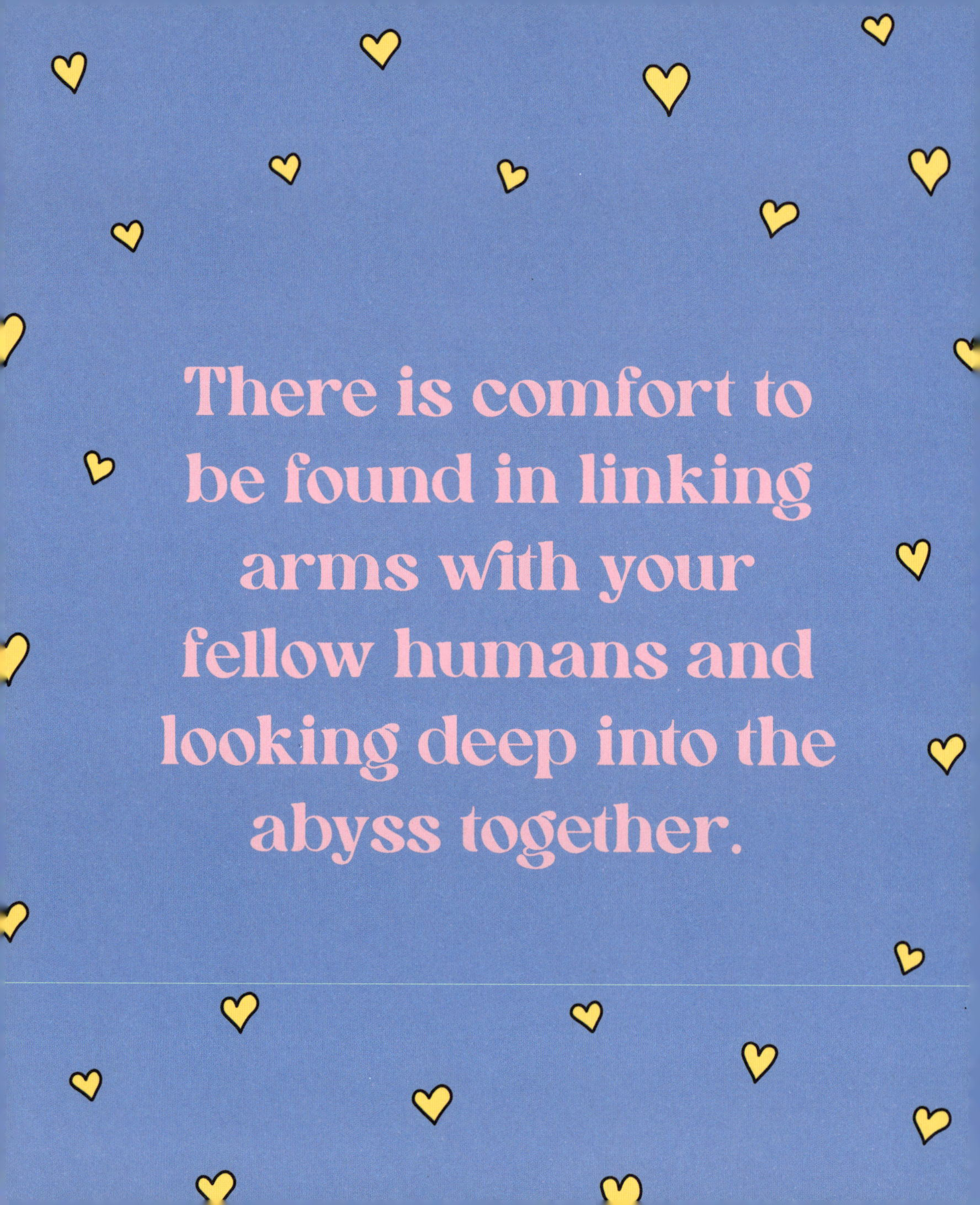
There is comfort to be found in linking arms with your fellow humans and looking deep into the abyss together.

with those I love – that the resulting sense of togetherness helps us survive. It's a common comparison to make, but think of it this way: in ecological communities, natural groupings of plants, animals and organisms share resources to build resilience and resistance to outside threats. Trees help each other stay alive through complex mycelium networks and humans are wired to do the same, by offering support and relief (both tangible and emotional) in the form of community. The alternative – focussing on individualism in the face of collective problems – will only serve to further isolate us and magnify our differences. No matter how tough things get (and there's a good chance they will get tougher) we do and will continue to have each other. And that's pretty comforting.

LOOK AT YOU
YOU
BIG
STAR
WONKY

Despite being a professional artist and illustrator, there are two things I cannot draw. One of them is a human hand (I've always insisted my characters' misshapen mittens are a creative decision!) and the other is a symmetrical star. I can draw them and redraw them all I like, but they always have weird little corners jutting out in the wrong directions. They are lopsided and messy, but still kind of cute.

Getting older has been a process of realising that the lopsided parts of myself that I was once bullied for – the parts I was once desperate to change – have (like my little stars) become the things that I'm most proud of as an adult. My sensitivity, while still a double-edged sword, has become something I depend on to express myself and connect with people. My femininity, which had me bullied and mocked for years as a child, now emboldens me to wear clashing floral prints, paint my nails and limp-wrist my way through challenging gym sessions.

I've also seen similar realisations in my friends and loved ones. With age comes the insight to view our imperfections as the things that make us shine against an otherwise dark backdrop. We may spend years fretting over all the ways we look, act, think and process things differently to others, until we eventually realise that it just doesn't matter. And what's more, when we all embrace being lopsided, comfortable and cute, it helps attract the right kind of people into our lives – the kind who see, understand and accept us.

With age comes the insight to view our imperfections as the things that make us shine against an otherwise dark backdrop.

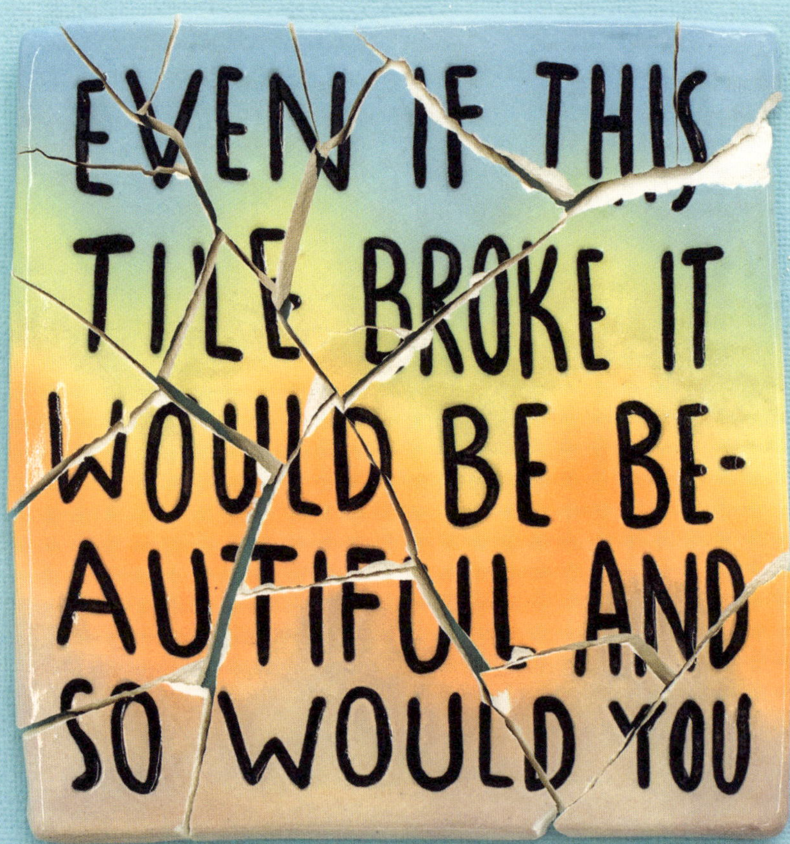
EVEN IF THIS
TILE BROKE IT
WOULD BE BE-
AUTIFUL AND
SO WOULD YOU

My personal experience with psychological collapse is like the Olympics or a US presidential election, in that it occurs every four years – usually due to a lovely combination of working too hard, drinking too much and ignoring my mental health in general. It might be surmised that breakdowns are a considerate (if inconvenient) way for our bodies and brains to tell us that we urgently need to reflect and reset.

I also find it hard to relate to anyone who hasn't had a good breakdown. It's probably why more than one member of my bridal party would list *Girl, Interrupted* as their favourite film. I've long believed that being broken down to nothing and having to build yourself back up again is one of the most human things in the world. And the sharing of that experience with others is one of the most connecting.

Admittedly, it would be easier to see the upside of a breakdown if it wasn't so painful and confronting while chest deep in one, but I'd

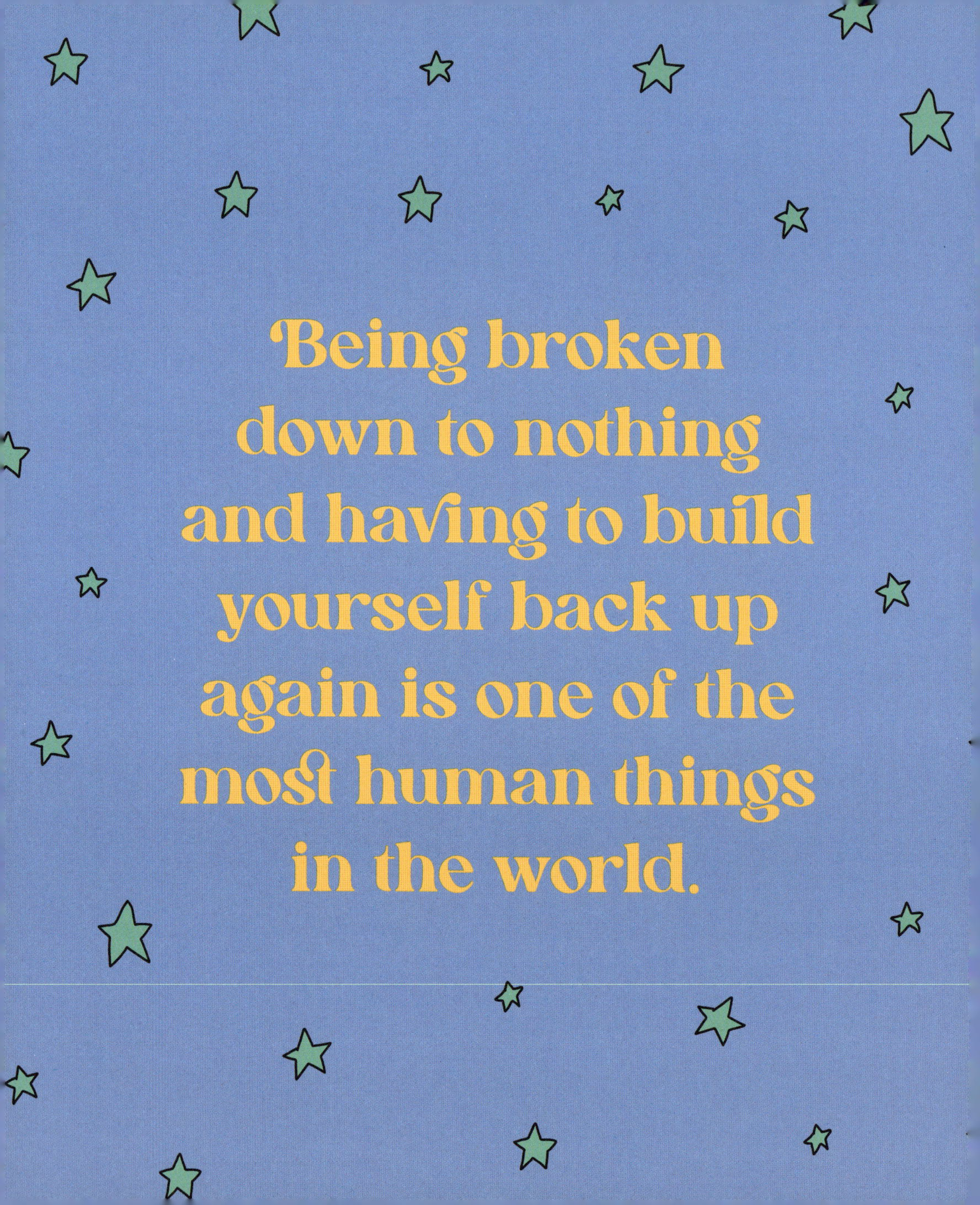
Being broken
down to nothing
and having to build
yourself back up
again is one of the
most human things
in the world.

argue that they're beautiful nonetheless. They have the potential to give us a new capacity for empathy. They can help us reconfigure our lives – to trace backwards and map forwards – rather than sail blindly to a destination unknown. They tend to remind us how fragile (and therefore precious) we are and, by extension, the tremendous care we need to take with ourselves.

A solid, bottom-of-the-barrel breakdown might very convincingly present itself as the end of the world, but it isn't; it's the opposite. It's a chance to let one version of ourselves go and another more tender, conscious and intentional version flourish. And that's pretty special.

IF YOU CAN RE-
AD THIS YOU A-
RE NO LONGER
A BABY BUT Y-
OU'RE STILL LOVED

Author's note: I'd like to apologise in advance to any unusually intelligent babies who can, in fact, read. Apparently, some can do so from as early as three-months old, which sounds fake, but that's what the internet tells me. If you are reading this as a baby, please know that I mean no offence.

It's interesting the way we collectively view all babies as deserving of love, care and gentle understanding. Of course, all babies *do* deserve these things, but isn't it a little strange that this default compassion and generosity seems to expire when we become adults?

If anything, babies who have learned to walk and talk, survived the perils of thirteen years at school, found jobs and scraped together a living in a world that sometimes works against them are especially deserving of our love, care and gentle understanding. Sure, grown-up babies need to take responsibility for their actions, but the world would be a more peaceful place if we viewed one another as the vulnerable children we once were. Because, whether we like it or not, many of us are only just recovering from our childhoods.

People often say you should imagine the audience naked when you're anxious about public speaking. That has never really worked for me, but something that *has* worked is imagining my audience as babies: gurgling, soiling their nappies and spitting up on themselves.

The next time you're feeling frustrated or angry with someone, try thinking of them as a toddler. It brings humour and understanding to a tense situation, because even when we mess up or lash out as adults, we're often the same as babies: hungry, tired, and just looking for someone to hold us and tell us we'll be okay.

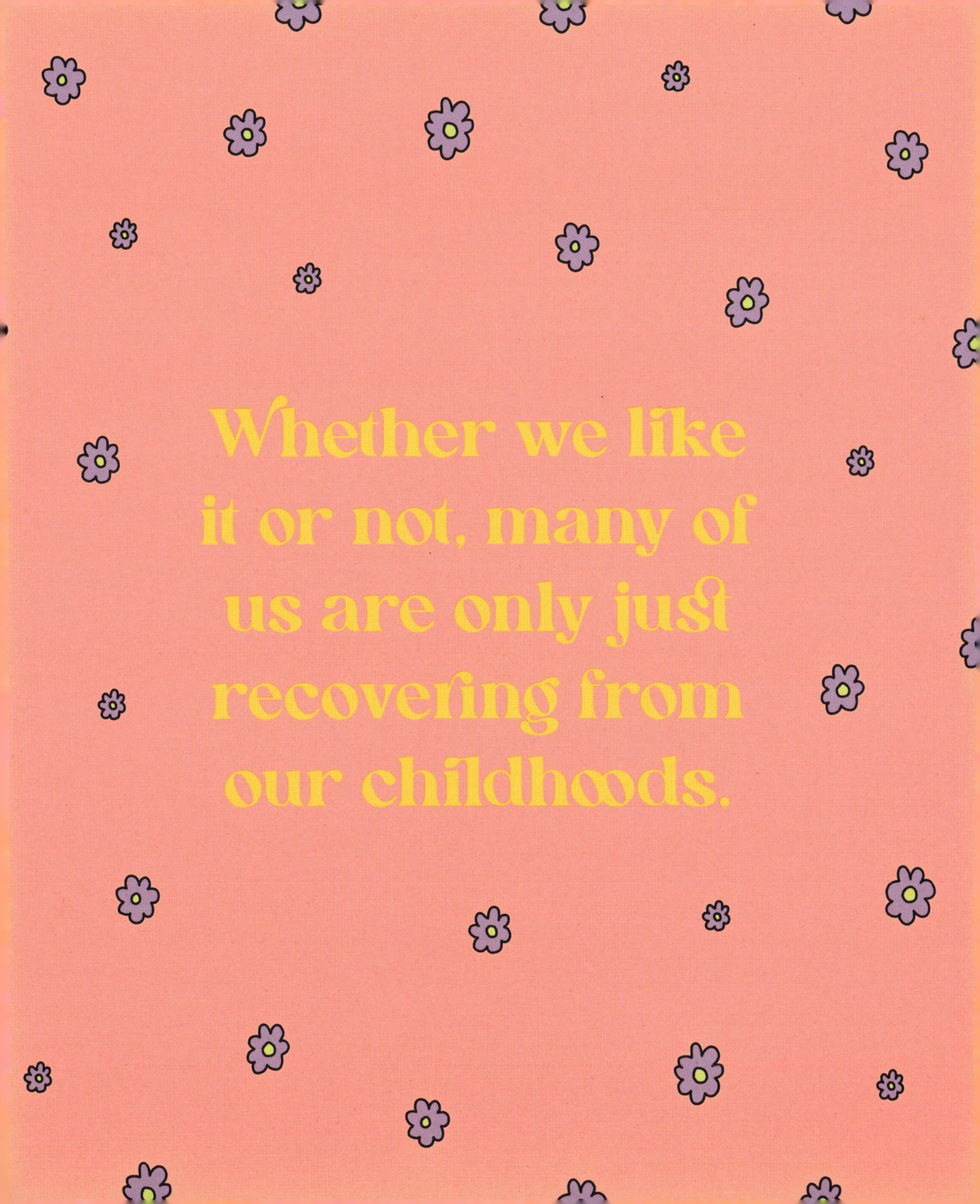
Whether we like it or not, many of us are only just recovering from our childhoods.

YOU EXIST
BEYOND Y-
OUR CIRCU-
MSTANCES

It can be hard to differentiate who we are from our circumstances. If we lose our job, we might feel unemployable. If we experience abandonment or rejection, we can see ourselves as unlovable. Things that happen to us often inform the way we view ourselves, but it's never the full picture.

Our circumstances certainly shape the people we are, but we also exist beyond them in a way that can't be impacted by anything external. Not to get all 'mindful' on you (I definitely am), but the one constant in our lives *is* our mind. If we're lucky (short of disease or injury) our mind is the only thing that we'll never be without, and the lens through which we always have, and always will, process our lives.

It therefore stands to reason that the gravitational centre of our existence is, in fact, *internal* – untouchable by whatever big, scary circumstances swirl around us.

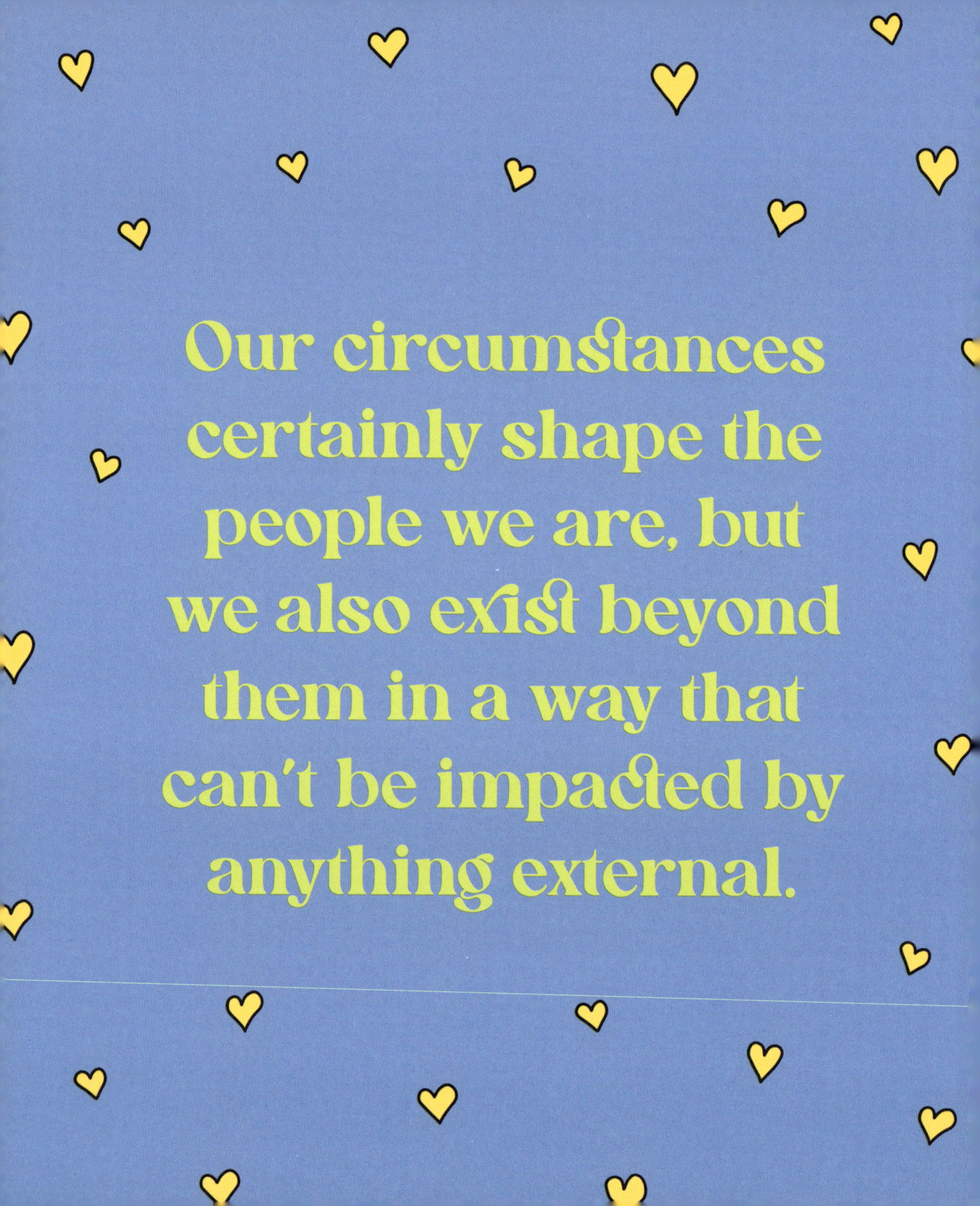
Our circumstances
certainly shape the
people we are, but
we also exist beyond
them in a way that
can't be impacted by
anything external.

Still, we can find ourselves caught up in the gravity wells of certain schools of thought and belief systems when we give them the power to dictate our joy and grief.

Even though I haven't come close to mastering it yet, try to remind yourself that much of what you need and depend on each day is already present within you, and that everyday setbacks can only shake your foundations when you allow them to take hold.

YOU ARE
THE YELL-
OW BIT
NOT
THE
PETALS

There is empowerment to be found in how we express ourselves externally – we do it through the way we dress and how we carry ourselves – but these expressions of self don't *equate* self.

Thanks to capitalism and a lifetime of conditioning, it is tough not to place our sense of value and identity on the things we and others can see: the petals. But sadly, at the end of the day, all petals eventually wilt and fall away. These colourful, pretty parts can be special, important and affirming, but they're not *who* we are. Most of the time, when a flower's petals fall to the ground, all that's left behind is the little yellow centre, attached to a largely unremarkable stalk. This is an easy concept to grasp but a difficult one to believe: the petals cannot *exist* without the yellow bit; the flowers themselves couldn't be pollinated without it. And, on fruit trees, the bit that's left behind is the part that turns into the fruit.

I like to believe our internal human existence is similar to these flowers, that our 'soul' (or whatever you want to call it) is the core of who we truly are and the rest is simply a way for us to communicate that sense of self to others. It's dangerous to place our worth in things that can be lost or taken away. A safer bet is to imagine ourselves without all the things we present to the world – physical beauty, clothes, belongings – and love whomever we find underneath.

There is empowerment to be found in how we express ourselves externally ... but these expressions of self don't *equate* self.

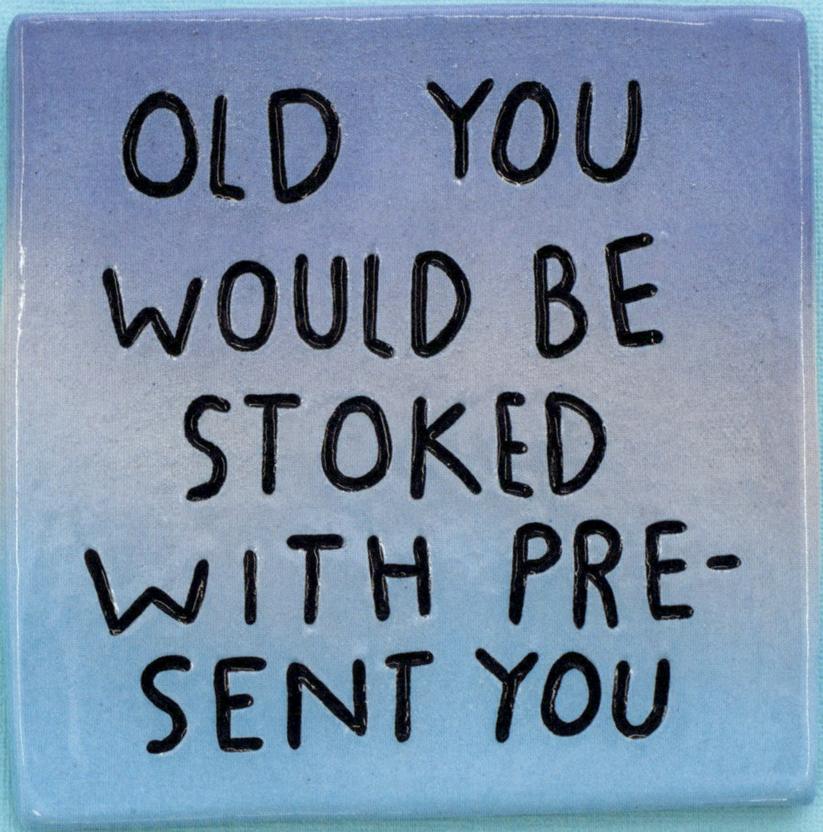

OLD YOU
WOULD BE
STOKED
WITH PRE-
SENT YOU

I often find that focussing on my younger self can be a great source of both groundedness and gratitude. There's no way that ten-year-old Sam (sitting alone and miserable at lunchtime) would've believed that one day he'd be writing a book, let alone that he'd make it through high school in one piece, find someone who loves him and enjoy his line of work.

In fact, he'd probably look at my life as it is now with a sense of wonder because it all just seemed so unlikely back then, when I felt unlovable and directionless, and all I saw for myself was a cold life of treading water. I still occasionally feel like this, but now the weather's a little warmer, I'm wearing flippers and there are people I love in the water with me.

We are taught to spend a lot of time thinking about our future selves, visualising how good things might be if and when we achieve certain goals. It's almost as if we feel safer existing in

Your present circumstances might not be perfect, but there are probably components already in place that you once hoped for.

our many potential realities than we do in the present. But, if we shift our perspective to that of our younger selves, there's a good chance we'd realise just how close we already are to that which we once felt was impossible. Your present circumstances might not be perfect – there may be lots you'd still like to change – but there are probably components already in place that you once hoped for.

It might feel easier to look towards the next hurdle than to pause mid-stride, turn around, and reflect on those you've already cleared, but when you do, you may just realise how stoked past you would be with present you.

NOT MIND-
ING IS BETT-
ER THAN N-
OT CARING

When we say we 'don't care' about an outcome, we're saying we don't place any value in it or the decision that came to it. We don't *care* what we have for dinner. We don't *care* who tags along on a day out. Whereas when we say we 'don't mind', we're giving ourselves and others more flexibility, freedom and acceptance – we don't *mind* what they pick for dinner; we don't *mind* who tags along. We are still invested heart and soul in something, but our peace and happiness is not *dependent* on it.

Sure, it's a simple shift in language – not unlike changing 'I have to do something' to 'I get to do something' – but what are our thoughts and views structured around if not language? Telling others that we don't *mind* lets them know that we care about their decisions, and are open to (and value) the ones they make.

Simply put, minding less frees us to care more. It allows us to live less bound to things outside of our control – to live life and pursue goals aligned with our values, safe in the knowledge that we'll be okay regardless of what happens. So, next time you feel the urge to tell someone that you 'don't care', try switching it out for its gentler alternative.

Telling others that we don't mind lets them know that we care about their decisions, and are open to (and value) the ones they make.

YOU ARE THE YELL-OW BIT
NOT
THE
PETALS

HAHAHAHA
HAHAHAHA
HAHAHAHA
HA OH DEAR

Comedy and pain are inextricably linked, whether it's laughing until we cry or crying until we laugh. This might be why, in the most challenging times of my life, I have looked to comedians for guidance and, yes, levity.

I've got what some would consider to be a dark sense of humour and I use it liberally to help process the gloomy stuff in life. When we're all being served an absolute smorgasbord of daily darkness, what are we supposed to do if not find the yummy, funny, light bits? In a world increasingly defined by illness, misinformation and chaos, laughter is one of the only things that *should* be contagious and, in my humble opinion, we should all have our minds set on becoming super spreaders.

I mean, what's not to love? A nervous chuckle in an awkward social situation? Great stuff. Someone calling themselves out with a self-deprecating joke? *Chef's kiss*. Laughing at

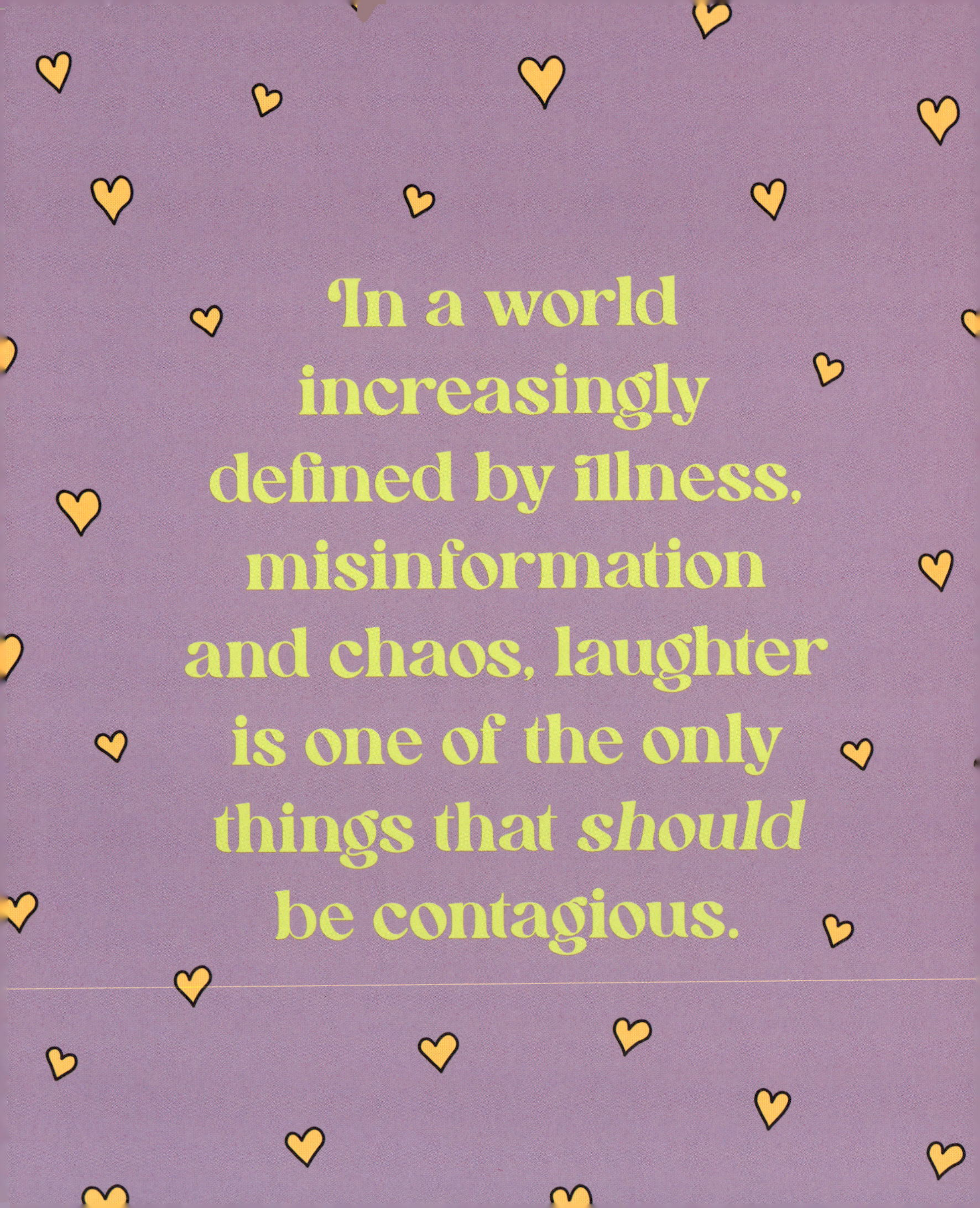
In a world
increasingly
defined by illness,
misinformation
and chaos, laughter
is one of the only
things that *should*
be contagious.

someone else's laughter in a crowded movie theatre? My idea of heaven. The cathartic laughter following a funny anecdote at a funeral? Straight-up healing shit. An inside joke with a close friend? The ultimate social bond.

When we're able to simultaneously acknowledge that something is bad, while also extracting the humour (however bleak) from it, we're in a much stronger position to process and, at the end of the day, cope with it. French playwright Jean Racine once said that 'Life is a comedy to those who think, a tragedy to those who feel.' The irony of life is that we both think *and* feel, and often at the same time.

IT REALLY IS
ALRIGHT NOT
TO HAVE AN
OPINION ON
EVERYTHING

Opinions are impossible to escape these days. We have millions of them at our fingertips and that number only multiplies on a daily basis. The internet gives a lot of us a platform to share our thoughts with the world and, while the compulsion to do so can be strong, the number of opinions we form is often greater than the number of subjects we're actually knowledgeable about.

Reading articles has given way to reading headlines. Healthy discussion has fallen by the wayside in favour of comment-section bloodbaths. For better or worse (mostly the latter), social media has become the great opinion equaliser, placing equal value on the views and opinions of faceless algorithm-generated bots and armchair extremists as it does scientists, academics and experts.

Having an opinion isn't helpful or productive when it's not an informed one, when it's anchored in reacting, posturing or chasing social status over truth and understanding. We simply don't have the time or capacity to be informed on *everything* (honestly, what a relief!). So the next time you find yourself standing on that virtual stage with a microphone in hand, try setting it down and listening to those with lived experiences instead, even if they're not standing in the spotlight.

Having an opinion
isn't helpful
or productive
when it's not an
informed one.

OUR LIGHT
WON'T HIT
THE STARS
FOR ANOTHER
HUNDRED YEARS

Indulge me for a moment here: I've read that if an alien life form lived on a planet one-hundred light-years away, with a giant telescope pointed directly at Earth, that alien would be watching human life in real time, but as it happened a hundred years ago.* It means that in the decade I am writing this, our alien friend would be watching the Jazz Age unfold, viewing life as it was in the 1920s. I mean, I'll likely die of old age (fingers crossed) before they even see my *birth*.

For some, this line of thinking could easily be a source of great anxiety, but I find it strangely comforting. It reveals just how big and mysterious the universe truly is. It makes me feel miniscule and inconsequential in all the best ways – like my very existence is a blip that won't be detectable until I'm long gone. Honestly, I'd much rather be a speck of dust coasting through the cosmos than some big, important life form with the weight of the universe on their shoulders.

*Magee, B. (2016) *Ultimate Questions*. Princeton University Press.

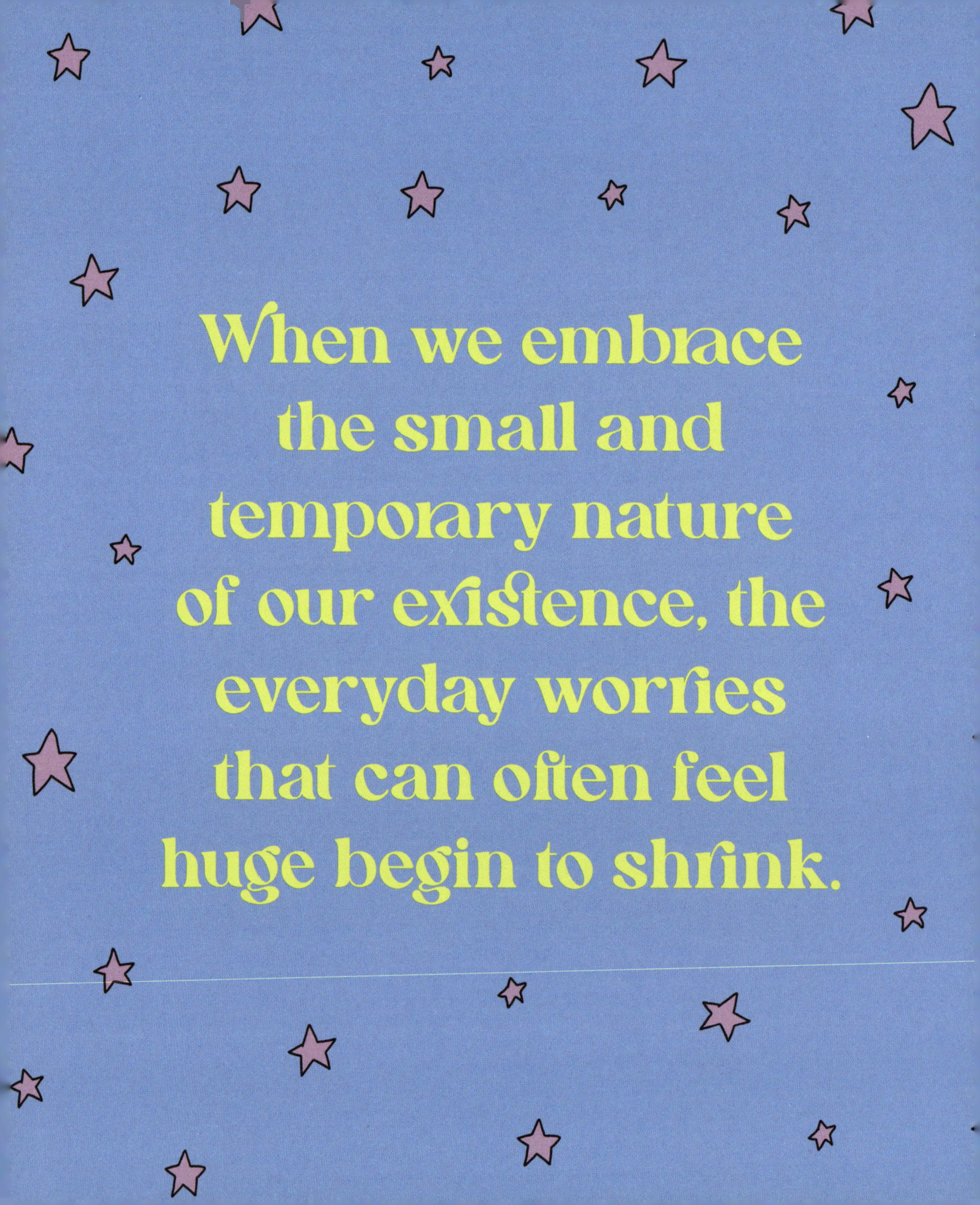

When we embrace the small and temporary nature of our existence, the everyday worries that can often feel huge begin to shrink.

A sunnier way of considering this might be to imagine that our lives will continue to exist long after we're gone, our happiest moments transformed into light that ripples out into the cosmos.

When we embrace the small and temporary nature of our existence, the everyday worries that can often feel huge begin to shrink. Situations or feelings that once seemed so permanent reveal themselves as largely insignificant, and surely there's a level of freedom to be found in that.

NOT EVERY CLOUD HAS A SILVER LI- NING AND THAT IS OKAY

I'm just going to say it: optimism can be unhelpful.

While I don't subscribe to a perpetual state of pessimism either, there *is* a certain relief (what they call a 'cold comfort') in accepting that bad things do, and will, in some capacity, continue to happen. Living with this kind of mindset isn't a sentence to life-long unhappiness; in my experience it can increase our capacity to appreciate positive things when they *do* happen.

If we spend our time anticipating *great* things for ourselves, the *good* things can feel like failures. We diminish the potential day-to-day humanity of life by the sheer virtue of it not being spectacular. Alternatively, when we make peace with less-ideal outcomes, and accept failure and rejection as possible, the *good* can feel *great*. We can be surprised by displays of unexpected kindness and feel more inclined to celebrate the little wins.

When we learn to expect scary things, they lose their power to frighten us. While the allure of optimism is understandable, the reality is that some clouds don't have a silver lining. They can be dark and stormy, stretching out as far as the eye can see, blurring into one another and blocking out the sun completely for days or weeks on end. This can be depressing if we're always decked out in our togs waiting for a chance to sunbake, but a great chance to work on ourselves if we're rugged up indoors – or to delight in the absurdity of it all, armed with an umbrella. Then, when the light eventually breaks through (because it does eventually break through), it'll feel all the more special.

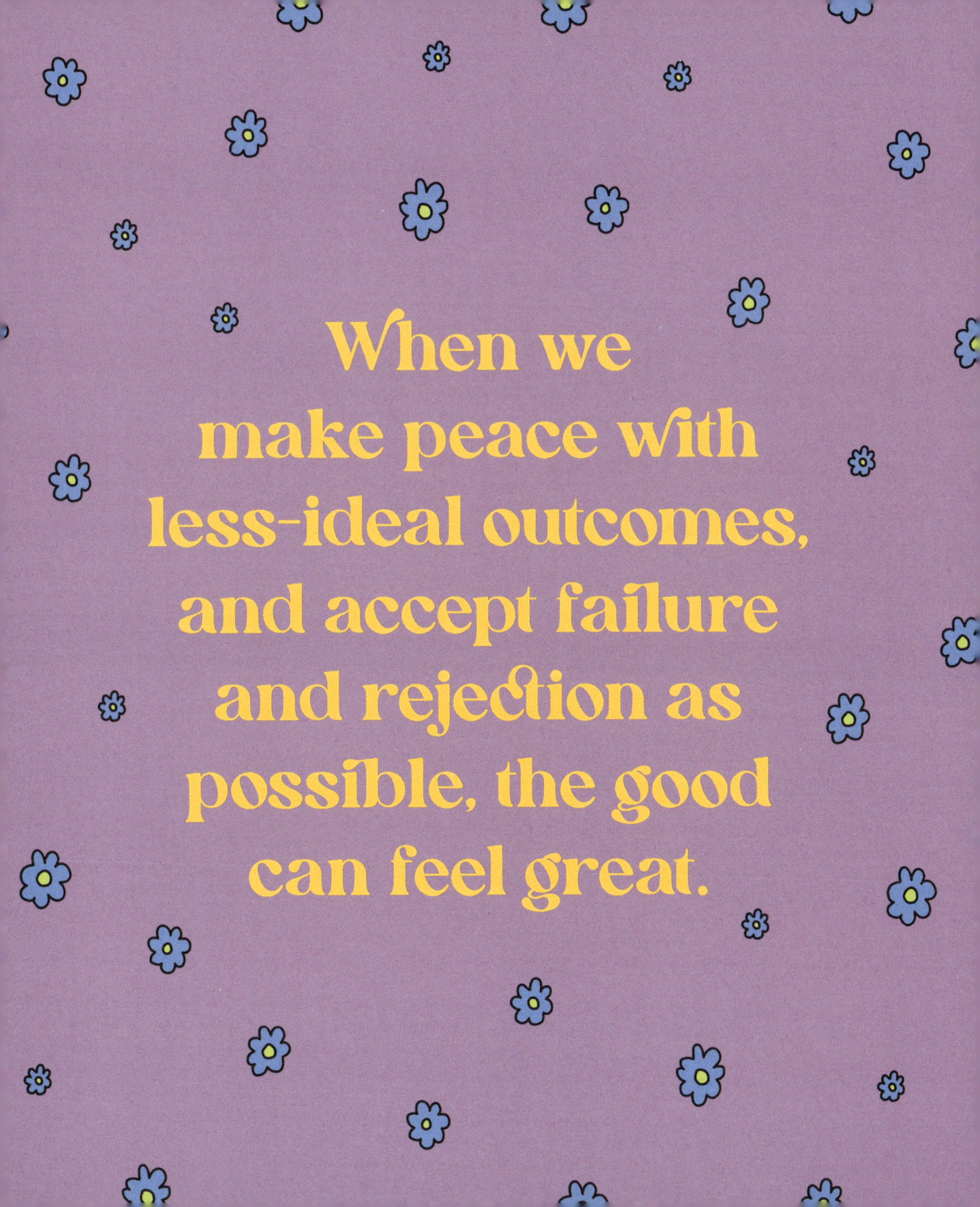
When we
make peace with
less-ideal outcomes,
and accept failure
and rejection as
possible, the good
can feel great.

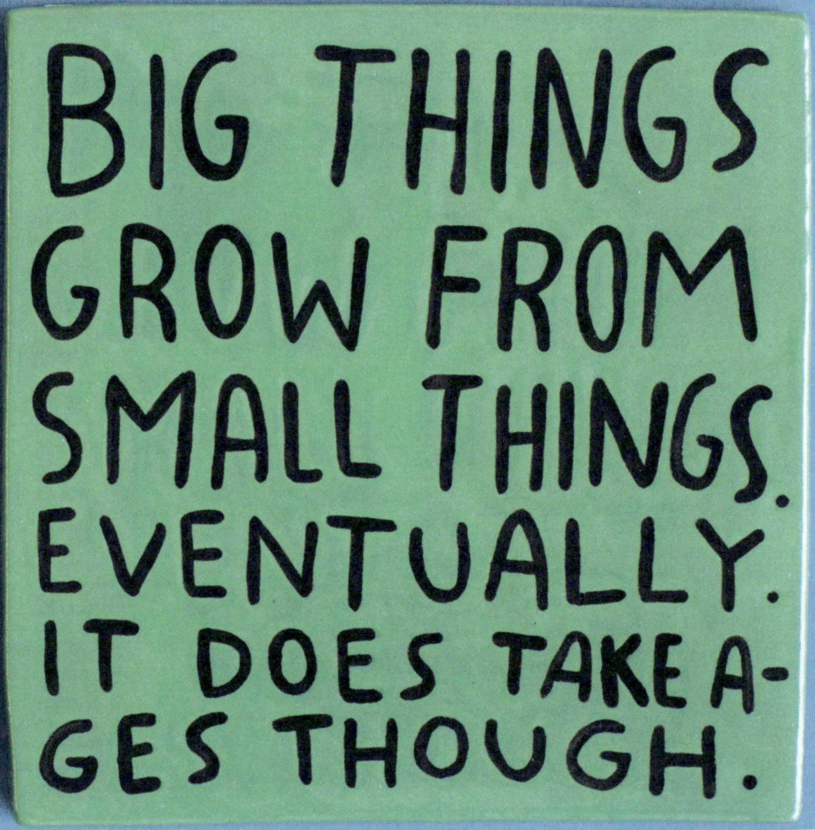

BIG THINGS
GROW FROM
SMALL THINGS.
EVENTUALLY.
IT DOES TAKE A-
GES THOUGH.

As a society, we don't spend enough time acknowledging how damn *long* everything takes to accomplish.

For instance, let's look at our mental health. Finding a good psychologist takes ages: it requires finding a good doctor with a sound understanding of mental illness, getting a referral, taking that referral to a nearby psychology clinic and then spending an unknowable amount of time on some elusive waitlist. And, after all that, the first psychologist you see most likely won't be a good fit, so the cycle starts over. When you *do* eventually find the right psychologist, the real marathon of healing begins, which can be a 'one-step-forward, ten-steps-back' kind of thing.

The same could be said for getting to a place in life where we enjoy our career. For some of us, it can take the better part of a decade (or often way more) of working in roles we have no real interest in. For others, it simply never

We don't spend
enough time
acknowledging
how damn long
everything takes
to accomplish.

happens. Creatives like me will be familiar with the sensation of pushing a small boulder up a big hill – unable to glimpse the top, struggling to work out whether a calm plateau is just over the next bump or still years away. Writing a play, putting on an exhibition, or getting a book published can take so long that many people are justifiably tempted to give up.

We've all heard the phrase that 'good things take time', but for a lot of us it's wrapped up with frustration as we try to soften the repeated blows of disappointment that come with existing in a goal-oriented society. Instead, I say we collectively work towards giving in and making peace with the often unremarkable journey itself, whether it be long or short. (Spoiler: it'll be long.)

THINGS TO LOOK FORWARD TO:

- YUMMY FOOD
- PRETTY SUNSETS
- KISSING STRANGERS

When there's nothing coming up on your calendar to look forward to, it can be helpful to think about all the years that stretch ahead of you, and all the potential little daily joys nestled among them.

Here are a few things, in no particular order, to add to your own list:

- Travelling somewhere new, even if it's not that far away.
- Eating something delicious.
- Discovering a dreamy new colour in a particularly striking sunset.
- Kissing a hot stranger at a dance party.
- Making a new friend.
- Connecting on a deeper level with existing friends.
- A day when you do absolutely nothing at all.

- Going for a walk and leaving your phone at home.
- Feeling relieved after a good cry.
- Watching a great new film or TV show.
- *Rewatching* a great film or TV show.
- The unexpected joy of a really good coffee paired with a comforting book.
- Not setting a morning alarm.
- Having an empty seat next to you on a long flight.
- Being paid promptly.
- Folding warm laundry.
- Finding an affordable outfit that fits just right.
- So many new songs.
- A baby laughing at you, then spitting up on themselves.

The unexpected joy of a really good coffee paired with a comforting book.

YOUR
THOUGHTS
YOU

No tool is more helpful for mental health than a well-constructed analogy. They calm me to no end. They allow me to communicate ideas that feel incommunicable.

The ocean and outer space are rich with analogical potential because they both contain depths beyond human reach (just like our minds!). The concept that waves are to thoughts what we are to the ocean has, I'm sure, been around for a very long time. For one thing, waves couldn't exist without the ocean, just as our thoughts couldn't exist without us. Waves are created through friction between wind and surface water, just as our thoughts tend to arise internally in relation to what is happening to us externally.

No matter how big, scary or potentially damaging a wave might seem, it will always retreat and disappear. No wave in the history of Earth has ever been permanent (though it's fun to imagine what that would look like) and

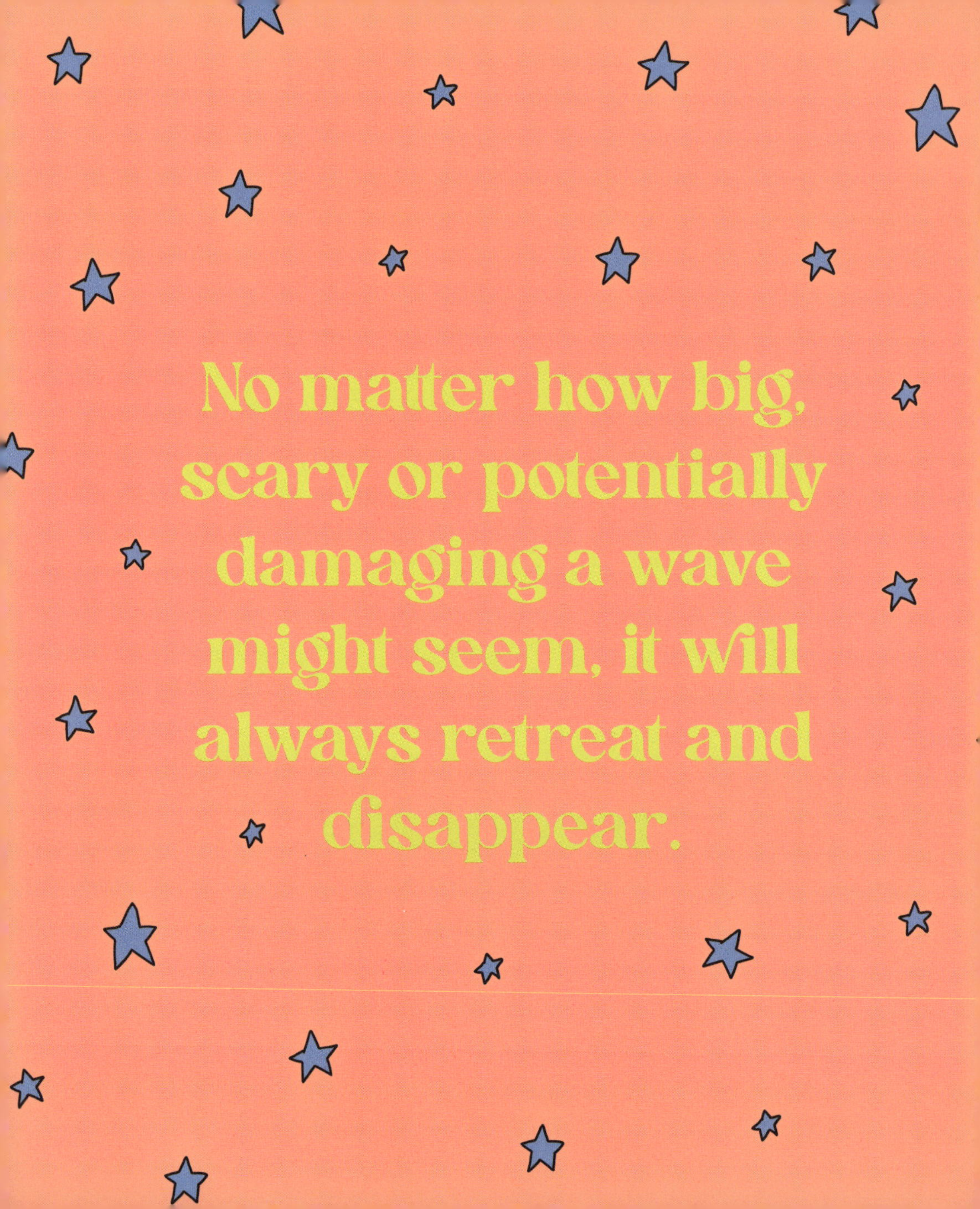
No matter how big,
scary or potentially
damaging a wave
might seem, it will
always retreat and
disappear.

no thought is permanent either. Even the big, scary, recurring thoughts will peak, curl over and disappear back to where they came from. Some people like to talk about learning to surf these thought waves, but I lack the stability and upper-body (read: mental) strength. Instead, I tend to get dumped by them (and wind up with sand in my crotch) or I dive beneath them, feeling them roll over my back as they crash in the distance.

Either way, focussing on the inherent impermanence of your thoughts goes a long way to alleviating their pressure. And thinking of yourself as the ocean will, eventually, help foster a deep and glimmering sense of calm, regardless of any storms on the horizon.

REST
YOU BEA-
UTIFUL
BUSY WEIRDO

I've always struggled to slow down, which my psychologist tells me is a method of avoidance. Between work, family, friends, hobbies, exercise and keeping the apartment somewhat presentable, there's not a lot of time for me to sit with myself and get, for lack of a better word, *existential*. Throw into the mix whatever activity I'm dressing up as 'self-care' during a given week and my life tends to take on a certain 'fast-forward' quality, like skipping through an old video tape, watching the characters glitch and lurch as they speed towards the end of their journey.

On some level, we know all too well that resting is important. We might equate it with taking the afternoon to binge-watch a particular show, or lying in bed and scrolling through social media. But, while watching TV or scrolling on our phones might help us slow down, they can still be forms of distraction (albeit calmer, more pleasant ones).

The real challenge for me is practising the elusive art of 'doing literally nothing'.

The idea of grinding to a halt terrifies me, not least because I fear it will give my heaving back-catalogue of unprocessed thoughts a solid chance to catch up. There's also the insidious idea that restful days are somehow wasted days – that, if I'm not constantly pushing something forward, everything will move on without me. But it's the whole carrot-on-the-stick thing – life moves as quickly as we do, and it doesn't go anywhere when we choose to stop running. At the end of the day, I think we all aspire to find fullness in an emptier schedule, to switch on our 'Out of Office' and *actually* not check our emails, to let our crowded minds slowly empty so that we might peek at the darkness left behind and grow comfortable with it.

It's okay to be busy. But it's important to rest too. Even if we're still learning how to do it.

On some level,
we know all too
well that resting
is important.

Support

AUSTRALIA

Beyond Blue
www.beyondblue.org.au

Lifeline
www.lifeline.org.au

1800 Respect
www.1800respect.org.au

QLife
www.switchboard.org.au/qlife

Mensline
www.mensline.org.au

Kids Helpline
www.kidshelpline.com.au

UK

SANEline
www.sane.org.uk

Switchboard
www.switchboard.lgbt

NEW ZEALAND

Lifeline
www.lifeline.org.nz

Need to Talk
Text or call 1737

OutLine
www.outline.org.nz

I Am Hope
www.iamhope.org.nz

USA / CANADA

Crisis Text Line
Text HOME to 741741

988 Suicide & Crisis Lifeline
www.988lifeline.org

Talk Suicide Canada
www.talksuicide.ca

Hope for Wellness Help Line
www.hopeforwellness.ca

Acknowledgements

Thanks to Brad, for loving me even when I make it hard, and being there to arrange the pieces when I drop something and it breaks. Michelle, for all the hugs and help. Bee, for being a great photographer and an even better friend. Chris, for generously lending your insights to this labour of love. Mark, for seeing the potential in a colourful ceramics-led book about mental health. Shannon, for understanding the heart of the book and helping my words make sense. And Mietta, for putting it all together so beautifully.

Harper *by* Design
An imprint of HarperCollins*Publishers*

HarperCollins*Publishers*
Australia • Brazil • Canada • France • Germany • Holland • India
Italy • Japan • Mexico • New Zealand • Poland • Spain • Sweden
Switzerland • United Kingdom • United States of America

HarperCollins acknowledges the Traditional Custodians of the land upon which we live and work, and pays respect to Elders past and present.

First published in Australia in 2023
by HarperCollins*Publishers* Australia Pty Limited
Gadigal Country
Level 13, 201 Elizabeth Street, Sydney NSW 2000
ABN 36 009 913 517
harpercollins.com.au

A catalogue record for this book is available from the National Library of Australia

ISBN 978 1 4607 6381 0 (hardback)
ISBN 978 1 4607 1611 3 (ebook)

Publisher: Mark Campbell
Publishing Director: Brigitta Doyle
Project Editor: Shannon Kelly
Designer: Mietta Yans, HarperCollins Design Studio
Photography: Bee Elton
Colour reproduction by Splitting Image Colour Studio, Wantirna, VIC
Printed and bound in China by 1010 Printing on 140gsm woodfree

8 7 6 5 4 3 2 1 23 24 25 26

About the Author

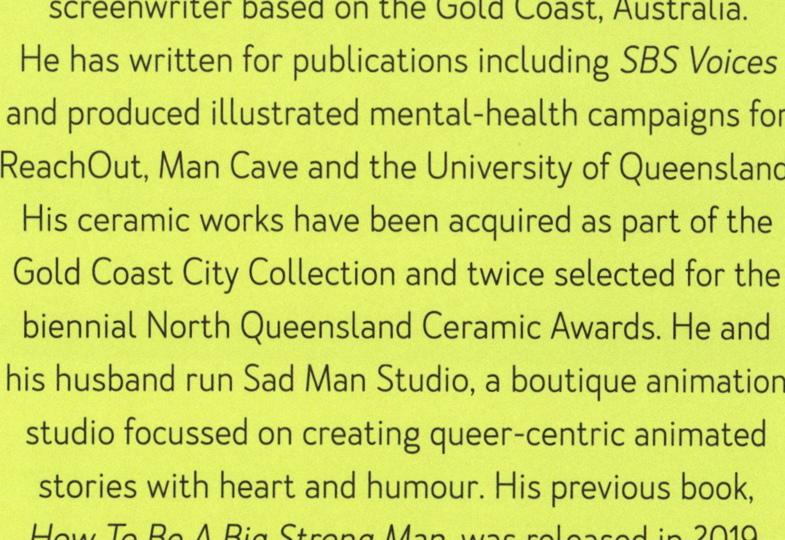

Samuel Leighton-Dore is an artist, author and screenwriter based on the Gold Coast, Australia. He has written for publications including *SBS Voices* and produced illustrated mental-health campaigns for ReachOut, Man Cave and the University of Queensland. His ceramic works have been acquired as part of the Gold Coast City Collection and twice selected for the biennial North Queensland Ceramic Awards. He and his husband run Sad Man Studio, a boutique animation studio focussed on creating queer-centric animated stories with heart and humour. His previous book, *How To Be A Big Strong Man*, was released in 2019.

@samleightondore
@thesmiletiles
www.sadmanstudio.com

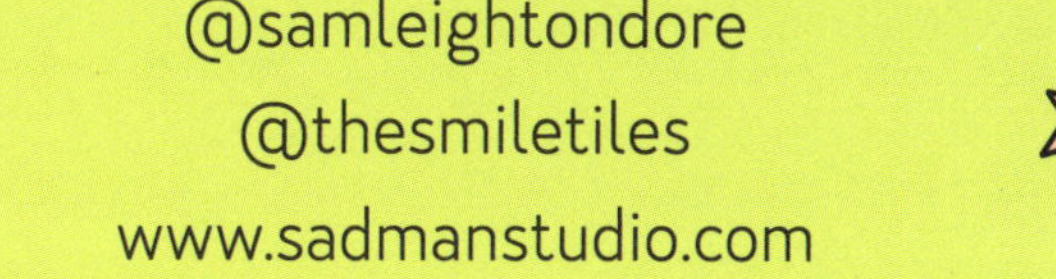

YOU EXIST BEYOND Y-OUR CIRCU-MSTANCES

YOU CAN DO IT* *GET THRO-UGH THIS DAY

YOUR BODY LOOKS STRON-G AND CAPA-BLE TODAY

LOOK WHO'S:
-UP AND ABOUT
-GIVING IT A CRACK
-BEING CUTE

THA THO REAL IT

YOUR THOUGHTS ≠ YOU

YOU DON'T HAVE TO READ THE NEWS TODAY

THAT SCARY THOUGHT IS REAL BUT IS IT TRUE?

NOT EVERY CLOUD HAS A SILVER LI-NING AND THAT IS OKAY

RE YOU UTI BUSY

YOU CAN DO IT* *GET THRO-UGH THIS DAY

WOW IT'S ALL A LOT HEY AT LEAST WE HAVE EACH OTHER

THEIR IDEA O-F SUCCESS D-OESN'T HAVE TO BE YOUR IDEA OF SUCCESS

HAHAHAHA HAHAHAHA HAHAHAHA HA OH DEAR

EVER ALRE ARD W BE SO

OLD YOU WOULD BE STOKED WITH PRE-SENT YOU

LOOK AT YOU BIG WONKY STAR

OUR LIGHT WON'T HIT THE STARS F-OR ANOTHER HUNDRED YEARS

CARE M-ORE MI-ND LESS

THE NO IN B

DON'T HUSTL-E SO HARD YO-U FORGET TO E-NJOY THIS WEI-RD FUN LITTLE LIFE YOU'VE BUILT

TELL SOMEONE YOU LOVE THAT THEY'RE HOT S-EXY SOFT GEN-TLE GONNA BE OK

IS IT ACTUA-LLY URGENT OR IS YOUR A-NXIETY TR-ICKING YOU?

IF YOU CAN RE-AD THIS YOU A-RE NO LONGER A BABY BUT Y-OU'RE STILL LOVED

THE NO IN B SC